THE STONES AND THE SCRIPTURES

Evangelical Perspectives

John Warwick Montgomery, General Editor

How Black Is the Gospel?
by Tom Skinner
The Unequal Yoke
by Richard V. Pierard
God, Sex and You
by M. O. Vincent, M.D.
Revolution and the Christian Faith
by Vernon C. Grounds
The Stones and The Scriptures
by Edwin M. Yamauchi

THE
STONES
AND THE
SCRIPTURES

Edwin M.Yamauchi

J. B. Lippincott Company / A Holman Book
Philadelphia and New York

Copyright © 1972 by Edwin M. Yamauchi
First edition
Printed in the United States of America

U.S. Library of Congress Cataloging in Publication Data

Yamauchi, Edwin M   birth date
  The Stones and The Scriptures.

  Bibliography: p.
  1. Bible—Antiquities. I. Title.
BS621.Y35   220.93   74–39483

ISBN–0–87981–002–5

To my sister
ALICE A. HIGA

Contents

Foreword   11
Acknowledgments   15
List of Illustrations   9
List of Abbreviations   10
Introduction   17

I. Mari, Nuzi, and Alalakh: *The Illumination of the Old
   Testament*   27
   A. Higher Criticism   27
   B. The Pre-Patriarchal Period   31
   C. The Patriarchs   36
   D. In and Out of Egypt   46
   E. The Conquest of the Promised Land   54
   F. Saul, David, and Solomon   64
   G. The Divided Kingdoms   71
   H. The Exile and the Post-Exilic Period   83

II. Ramsay Vs. The Tübingen School: *The Confirma-
   tion of the New Testament*   92
   A. The Tübingen School and Form Criticism   92
   B. Jesus of Nazareth   98
   C. Paul the Missionary   112
   D. The Early Church   121

III. Qumran and the Essenes: *The Dead Sea Scrolls*   126
   A. Discoveries and Purchases   126
   B. Dating the Finds   129
   C. Old Testament Manuscripts   129
   D. Sectarian Documents   132
   E. Excavations at Khirbet Qumran   134
   F. The Essene Identification of the Qumran Sect   136

7

G. Implications for New Testament Studies 137
H. The Teacher of Righteousness and Jesus of
   Nazareth 140

IV. Fragments and Circles: *The Nature of the
   Evidence* 146
A. The Fragmentary Nature of the Evidence 146
1. *The Fraction That Has Survived* 146
2. *The Fraction That Has Been Surveyed* 148
3. *The Fraction That Has Been Excavated* 149
4. *The Fraction That Has Been Examined* 151
5. *The Fraction That Has Been Published* 154

B. Overlapping Circles of Evidence 158
C. The Argument from Silence 160
D. Archaeology vs. Literary Criticism? 163
E. A Final Word 164

Selected Bibliography 167
Notes 174
Indexes:
   Modern Names 193
   Ancient Names 197
   Places 201
   Subject 203
   Scriptures 205

List of Illustrations

Figure

1. Map of Mesopotamia 19
2. Map of Palestine and Trans-Jordan 23
3. Cuneiform Tablet with the Flood Story 33
4. Pottery of the 13th Century B. C. from Hazor 49
5. Ivory Fragments from Ahab's Palace at Samaria 51
6. The Tribute of Jehu, King of Israel, before Shalmaneser 53
7. Bronze, Bone and Iron Arrow-Heads from Lachish 55
8. Inscribed Ostracon from Lachish 61
9. The Cyrus Cylinder 79
10. The Pool of Siloam 101
11. The Synagogue at Capernaum 103
12. The Church of the Holy Sepulchre 105
13. Ossuaries from Dominus Flevit on the Mount of Olives 107
14. The Roman Agora at Athens 109
15. The "Bema" at Corinth 117
16. The Dining Room at Qumran 135
17. The Cemetery at Qumran 137
18. Overlapping Circles of Evidence 158

List of Abbreviations

AJA	*American Journal of Archaeology*
AOTS	*Archaeology and Old Testament Study* ed. D. Winton Thomas
BA	*The Biblical Archaeologist*
BASOR	*Bulletin of the American Schools of Oriental Research*
BJRL	*Bulletin of the John Rylands Library*
DOTT	*Documents from Old Testament Times* ed. D. Winton Thomas
IEJ	*Israel Exploration Journal*
JAOS	*Journal of the American Oriental Society*
JBL	*Journal of Biblical Literature*
JBR	*Journal of Bible and Religion*
JNES	*Journal of Near Eastern Studies*
KJV	King James Version
LXX	Septuagint
MS	Manuscript
MT	Masoretic Text
NTS	*New Testament Studies*
PEQ	*Palestine Exploration Quarterly*
QS	*Quarterly Statement of the Palestine Exploration Fund*
RSV	Revised Standard Version

Foreword

Across the centuries the Christian church has faced two perennial challenges: the maintenance of a pure testimony, and the application of revealed truth to the total life of man. Though these two tasks interlock (since application of the truth is impossible if the truth is lost, and truth without application stands self-condemned), theology has generally devoted itself now to the one, now to the other, and the cause of Christ has suffered from the imbalance. "These ought ye to have done, and not to leave the other undone" stands as a perpetual judgment over the church's history.

Today's theology and church life display such deleterious polarization in an especially gross manner. At the liberal end of the theological spectrum, efforts to become "relevant" have succeeded so well that the church has become indistinguishable from the ideological and societal evils she is supposed to combat. Among the fundamentalists, in contrast, God's revealed truth often serves as a wall to block the church off from the live issues and compelling challenges of a world in crisis. Relevance without truth, or truth without relevance: these dual schizophrenias go far in explaining why contemporary man finds it easy to ignore the Christian message.

Evangelical Perspectives is a series of books designed specifically to overcome these false dichotomies. Historic Christian theology—the Christianity of the Apostles' Creed, of the Protestant Reformation, and of the eighteenth-century Evangelical Revival—is taken with full seriousness, and is shown to be entirely compatible with the best of contemporary scholarship. Contributors to this series are united in rejecting the defensive posture which has so often created the impression that new knowledge poses a genuine threat to the Christian gospel. Axiomatic to the present series is the conviction that new discoveries serve but to confirm and deepen the faith once delivered to the saints.

At the same time, those participating in this project find little comfort in the reiteration of ancient truth for its own sake. Our age faces staggering challenges which can hardly be met by the repetition of formulas—certainly not by the negativistic codes of a fundamentalism which tilts against windmills that have long since fallen into decay. The race problem, social revolution, political change, new sexual freedom, the revival of the occult, the advent of the space age: these are areas of modern life that demand fresh analysis on the basis of the eternal verities set forth in the Word of One who is the same yesterday, today, and forever.

Out of the flux of the current theological situation nothing but flux appears to be emerging. What is needed is a firm foundation on which to build an all-embracing and genuinely relevant theological perspective for the emerging twenty-first century. The authors of the present volumes are endeavoring to offer just such a perspective—an *evangelical* perspective, a perspective arising from the biblical evangel—as the one path through the maze of contemporary life.

It is the hope of the editor that upon the solid Reformation base of a fully authoritative Scripture, the present series will offer its readers the Renaissance ideal of the Christian as *uomo universale*. Such an orientation could revolutionize theology in our time, and ground a new age of commitment and discovery comparable to that of the sixteenth century. As in that day, new worlds are opening up, and just as a religious viewpoint reflecting the dying medieval age was unable to meet the challenge then, so today's secular theologies are incapable of pointing the way now. The Christ of the Bible, through whom all without exception have been created and redeemed: he alone is Way, Truth, Life—and Perspective!

JOHN WARWICK MONTGOMERY
General Editor

Acknowledgments

I would like to thank Dr. G. Douglas Young, director of the American Institute of Holy Land Studies, for his many kindnesses to myself and my family when we were in Israel in 1968. I especially appreciated the informed guidance of Dr. Anson Rainey of Tel Aviv University on field trips to numerous mounds and excavation sites. The lectures on archaeology by Dr. Moshe Kochavi of the Hebrew University were most rewarding.

For the high privilege of participating in the excavation at Jerusalem my warm thanks go to Professor Benjamin Mazar of the Hebrew University. I must also thank Miss Sylvie Nisbet of London for her infectious enthusiasm on the "dig." I am grateful to Dr. and Mrs. Saul Weinberg of the University of Missouri for allowing me to take part in their excavation at Tel Anafa in northern Israel.

For their willingness to read this manuscript and to offer suggestions, I am indebted to Professor James L. Kelso of Pittsburgh Theological Seminary, to Professor E. Jerry Vardaman of the Southern Baptist Theological Seminary, to Professor Ronald Youngblood of Bethel Theological Seminary, and to Professor Bastiaan Van Elderen of Calvin Theological Seminary. Any errors that remain are, of course, the author's responsibility.

For permission to use certain photographs, acknowledgment is made in the captions to the British Museum. Unless otherwise indicated, the photos are black-and-white prints made from slides taken by the author. I am indebted to the Audio-Visual Department of Miami University (Oxford, Ohio) for the preparation of the maps.

For permission to quote from their journals, I am thankful to the editors and publishers of: 1) articles by W. W. Hallo and Paul W. Lapp in *The Biblical Archaeologist*; 2) an article by H. H. Rowley in the *Bulletin of the John Rylands Library*; 3) W. F. Albright in the *Bulletin of the American Schools of Oriental Research*; 4) an article by W. W. Gasque in the *Evangelical Quarterly*; 5) a review by M. Avi-Yonah in the *Israel Exploration Journal*; 6) articles by H. H. Rowley and M. Smith in the *Journal of Biblical Literature*; 7) an article by G. Ernest Wright in the *Journal of Bible and Religion*; 8) an article by A. T. Olmstead in the *Journal of Near Eastern Studies*; and 9) an article by A. R. Millard in the *Tyndale Bulletin*.

For permission to cite extended passages from their publications my thanks go to:

1) Abingdon Press for citations from *The Bible in Modern Scholarship*, ed. J. Philip Hyatt (Nashville: Abingdon Press, 1965), pp. 41–42, 307, 319.

2) Baker Book House for citations from Adolf Deissmann, *Light from the Ancient East* (Grand Rapids: Baker Book House, 1965), pp. 80, 270, 354, 440.

3) Thomas Nelson & Sons for citations from *Documents from Old Testament Times*, ed. D. Winton Thomas (New York: Harper and Brothers, 1958), pp. 48, 55, 60, 67, 79–80, 93, 196, 210, 232.

4) McGraw-Hill Book Co. for citations from W. F. Albright, *History, Archaeology, and Christian Humanism* (copyright 1964 by W. F. Albright. Used with permission of McGraw-Hill Book Company.), pp. 32, 35, 265–66, 309.

INTRODUCTION

Archaeology is concerned with the recovery of the remains of ancient civilizations. In some cases these remains have always been visible: the Colosseum in Rome, the Parthenon in Athens, the Pyramids in Giza. A far greater portion have been buried by the debris of successive generations and have been uncovered in recent times by the archaeologist's "spade." As many discoveries are quite unexpected, archaeology is an exciting occupation.

For the reconstruction of prehistoric periods, the service rendered by archaeology in recovering artifacts is of paramount importance. For the periods after 3,000 B.C. when writing was invented, archaeology plays a supportive role in historical research. The discovery of texts inscribed in stone, on papyri, or potsherds, is the archaeologist's prize—far more valuable than any gold he might chance to find.

The evidence provided by archaeology is valuable for several reasons. Tangible objects make vivid the life setting of the ancient peoples. In contrast to most historical traditions which are concerned with the fortunes of kings and warriors, the common cooking pot informs us of the humble life of the housewife. Though the royal Egyptian and Assyrian texts that have been discovered cannot be described as disinterested evidence (many are quite transparent propaganda), they do provide us with a view of the biblical world which is more "historical"—from a secular historian's point of view—than the spiritual perspective of the biblical writers. For example, we should never have guessed the importance of Omri or of Herod the Great, to their contemporaries, from the scant notice given to them in the Scriptures. This is not to say that the biblical analysis is less true, but only to acknowledge that it is selective.

Although archaeology in its descriptive phase deals with concrete objects and employs exact measurements, we cannot claim that it is an exact science. Its interpretive aspects involve too many judgments of probabilities to secure the certainty of chemical experiments. On the other hand, certain principles of excavation command general acceptance, so that Albright can say of Palestinian archaeologists:

> The writer has known many such scholars, but he recalls scarcely a single case where their religious views seriously influenced their results. Some of these scholars were radical critics; still others were more conservative critics, like Ernst Sellin; others again were thorough-going conservatives. But their archaeological conclusions were almost uniformly independent of their critical views.[1]

As an indication of the purely humanistic motivation of recent archaeology, one may note that the director of a recent expedition in Israel was a Buddhist from Japan.

It is not to be denied, however, that interest in the relevance of archaeology for the Bible was a primary initiating factor and is still one of the chief motivating elements in the support of excavations today. Indeed, a popular notion exists that "archaeology has proved the Bible." There is truth to this aphorism (as we shall see), but it needs to be

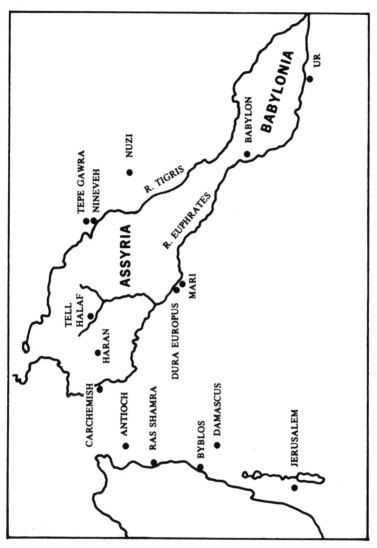

1. Outline map of Mesopotamia and Syria.

understood properly. If by "proof" is meant irrefutable evidence that everything in the Bible happened "just so," this "proof" cannot be provided by archaeology.[2]

There are a number of striking cases where specific passages have been doubted (it is a rare passage that has not been questioned by some critic) and have been directly confirmed. There are many more items and areas which have afforded a general illumination of biblical backgrounds, making the narratives more credible and understandable. Finally, there are some cases which—though they do not irrefutably prove that the Bible contains mistakes, as some critics may claim—certainly do require the believer to admit his inability to resolve difficulties without benefit of additional data. In such situations the evangelical recalls the numerous past instances in which the resolution of biblical problems has been impossible for one generation but readily available to those benefiting from later discoveries, and he holds fast by faith to his Lord's view of Scripture as that book "every word" of which "proceeded out of the mouth of God" (Matt. 4:4, quoting Deut. 8:3). As D. J. Wiseman, professor of Assyriology at the University of London, has affirmed:

> When due allowance has been paid to the increasing number of supposed errors which have been subsequently eliminated by the discovery of archaeological evidence, to the many aspects of history indirectly affirmed or in some instances directly confirmed by extra-biblical sources, I would still maintain that the historical facts of the Bible, rightly understood, find agreement in the facts culled from archaeology, equally rightly understood, that is, the majority of errors can be ascribed to errors of interpretation by modern scholars and not to substantiated "errors" of fact presented by the biblical historians. This view is further strengthened when it is remembered how many theories and interpretations of Scripture have been checked or corrected by archaeological discoveries.[3]

By its very nature archaeological evidence is fragmentary,

often disconnected, and always with the exception of texts—mute and materialistic. Far more than our need of these materials for an understanding of the Bible is our need of the Bible for an understanding of the materials. According to the Bible, Jehovah's revelation to Israel in the Old Testament, and Jesus' sacrificial death and resurrection in the New Testament, are the issues of paramount concern. Mortimer Wheeler has quipped that archaeology may find Diogenes' tub but miss Diogenes. Archaeology may find a ruined altar or an empty tomb, but these pale in the light of a transcendent Jehovah and a risen Christ. Their ultimate importance lies in the fact, stressed by Christ himself, that the truth of "earthly things" in God's Word leads directly to confidence in its "heavenly" content (John 3:12).

We may be grateful that excavations have provided a mass of evidence for the religious environments of the Old and the New Testaments. This has helped us both to recognize elements common to Judaism, Christianity, and rival religions, and rightly to appreciate the unique contributions of the Judeo-Christian faith.

It cannot be too strongly emphasized that since the biblical revelation claims to be a revelation of God acting in history —and not a revelation through cult or myth—a proper understanding of the historical background of the Bible has maximal significance for the theologian. André Parrot, the distinguished excavator of Mari, stresses this point:

As is well-known, certain currents of theological thought profess towards history an attitude almost of disdain. According to them, precise facts concerning the behavior of individuals have only a very minor importance. It is therefore pointless to attempt to give an exact date, or to go more closely into some train of political events. What matters, we are told, is the Word, and the Word alone. But how are we to understand it without setting it against its proper chronological, historical and geographical background? How are blunders to be avoided if our interpretation treats a given situation completely *in vacuo,* and without first attempting to define its exact contours?[4]

In his book on biblical archaeology Millar Burrows has argued: "Religious truth is one thing: historical fact is another. Neither necessarily presupposes or accompanies the other."[5] Now it is quite true that a work such as the Babylonian Chronicle may give us an accurate historical record but also present a religious perspective that is false— that is, from the Judeo-Christian perspective. Many have also argued that the Scriptures may err in historical detail without affecting theological verities.[6]

If by "error" one means a lack of precision in the transmission or translation of the biblical traditions, this is readily granted. A missionary may very well succeed in conveying the Gospel to the murderous Auca Indians of Ecuador by the use of his own imperfect translation. If, on the other hand, the claim of critics that the Old Testament books are generally late and untrustworthy, that the Gospels and the Acts are unreliable, that the so-called Pauline Epistles are not Pauline, etc. is given credence, faith in the truth of Scriptures is completely eroded.

It is well-known that the so-called "scientific" criticism of the Bible which arose in Germany in the nineteenth century and which eventually flooded British and American universities and seminaries has had precisely this effect. We can see that such criticism is far from objective. Its sources are to be found, *inter alia,* in the presuppositions of Hegelian philosophy and in evolutionary theories as to how Judaism and Christianity "must have developed."

In the United States in the early twentieth century the reaction to this attack on the integrity of the Bible developed into the fundamentalist movement. At its best, fundamentalism sought to conserve the essentials of orthodox Christiani-

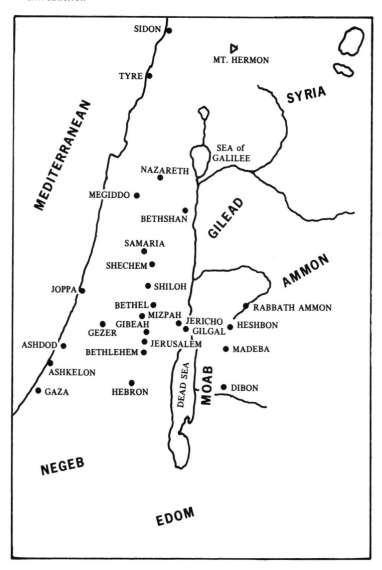

2. Outline map of Palestine and Trans-Jordan.

ty; at its worst, it attempted to do this by appeals to emotion and by an anti-intellectual rejection of critical scholarship. Fundamentalists in general welcomed the positive results of archaeology, but at times they abused such results by glossing over problems and by claiming more "proof" than the evidence has justified. The claim was made in one conservative handbook that Abraham's existence has been vouched for by written documents. The name "Abraham" or variants of it have indeed been found, but it is clear that they do not refer to the biblical Abraham. The occurrence of biblical names in contemporary documents supports their authenticity but does not "prove" the existence of the biblical characters unless the context of the documents demands such identification.

Although the results of archaeology may be overpressed by zealous but uninformed defenders of the faith, no one can gainsay the fact that particularly in the last forty years the general results of archaeology have made scholars more respectful of the historicity of ancient traditions, whether classical or biblical. G. Ernest Wright in a recent essay notes this:

It is indeed true that archaeology has revolutionized our attitude toward biblical historical traditions. A previous generation of scholars was inclined to make skepticism, an important element in historical method, an almost primary ingredient in the conclusions drawn for use of the method. Today most of us take a far more positive line, and are inclined to give a tradition the benefit of the doubt unless there is evidence to the contrary; this is a basic and all-important scholarly shift in viewpoint, and archaeology is its cause.[7]

The unmistakable shift toward a conservative view may be illustrated by comparing the views expressed by W. F. Albright on Genesis 14 in an article published in 1918 and in another article published in 1961. In the earlier article Albright regarded the chapter as a political pamphlet composed about 500 B.C., without historical foundation and borrowed from extant legends or invented.[8] Some forty years later Albright asserts that his studies "have established the absolute antiquity of the contents of the chapter and have shown that it is strewn with indications of a very archaic verse tradition. . . ."[9]

It is in large measure the work and influence of Albright himself, beginning with his work with the American Schools of Oriental Research in Jerusalem, and continuing with his teaching at Johns Hopkins University in Baltimore that has brought about a more positive attitude toward the Scriptures. The so-called "Baltimore" school of Albright has produced an impressive array of productive scholars: G. Ernest Wright and Frank Moore Cross, Jr. of Harvard, George E. Mendenhall of the University of Michigan, John Bright of Union Theological Seminary in Virginia, etc. Their emphasis on archaeology as opposed to the more skeptical literary criticism of German scholars has not always been warmly welcomed. A recent review harshly excoriates the Albright approach as "pseudorthodoxy" (sic), and as an obstacle to progress in Old Testament studies.[10] G. Ernest Wright has complained that his work, *Biblical Archaeology,* "has simply been labeled in more than one German review as poorly informed fundamentalism!"[11]

Evangelicals, characterized by a high view of the inspiration of the Scriptures without the antipathy to critical scholarship characteristic of fundamentalists, have welcomed the positive contributions of archaeology—with, however, an awareness of its limitations. A nucleus of evangelical scholars, such as F. F. Bruce in New Testament studies and D. J. Wiseman in the Near Eastern field, have demonstrated that it is possible to combine evangelical piety with scholarship.

The Stones and The Scriptures

The following work, written by one who is committed to the historic Christian faith, seeks to summarize, albeit in selective fashion, the archaeological evidence and its bearings upon the Scriptures. It seeks to face the complexities of problem areas and to offer some suggestions as to the perspective in which some of these difficulties may be viewed. The writer has sought to lay stress upon the discoveries of the last decade. Unhappily for the complacency of such writers on archaeology, so rapid is the flow of discoveries that statements made in this book may be obsolete by the time they are printed! But, hopefully, the general outlines of archaeological interpretation and the developmental trends in this fascinating field will have been accurately surveyed.

I

MARI, NUZI AND ALALAKH:
The Illumination of the Old Testament

Is the Old Testament a patchwork of popular folk-tales and legends? Have archaeologists found evidence of the biblical flood? Are the stories of the patriarchs—Abraham, Isaac, and Jacob—credible? Have the walls of Jericho which "tumbled down" before Joshua been found? Are there any references in non-biblical sources to events recorded in the Old Testament?

A. Higher Criticism

The widespread notion, found for example in college text books, that the Old Testament is a crazy quilt of unreliable legends owes its genesis to a discipline known as "higher" criticism. "Higher" or literary criticism is the study which attempts to determine the questions of the authorship, of the date, and of the composition of any literary text on the basis of vocabulary, style, and consistency. "Lower" or textual criticism, on the other hand, seeks to ascertain the original text by comparing manuscripts and ancient versions.

Modern literary criticism first began with the epochal work

of Homeric criticism by F. A. Wolf in 1795.[1] In biblical studies higher criticism received its classic exposition in 1878 in the work of Julius Wellhausen. The latter's "documentary" hypothesis, in contrast to the tradition of Mosaic authorship, analyzed the Pentateuch (the first five books of the Old Testament) as a work which had been woven together from late sources by anonymous editors. He called the hypothetical documents which had been stitched together J for Jehovah, E for Elohim, D for Deuteronomy, and P for the Priestly Code. These strands were assigned dates ranging from the ninth century B.C. for J to the sixth century B.C. for P on the basis of Wellhausen's concept of the evolution of Israel's religion. According to this viewpoint, which was influenced by Darwin and by Hegel, the religion of the Hebrews evolved at first into a national henotheism (the worship of one god from among many gods) and only much later in the time of the literary prophets and the Exile into an ethical monotheism.

Theoretically one may analyze a document into various component parts without necessarily casting doubt on its authenticity. In practice, however, higher criticism almost invariably resulted in a negative attitude toward the biblical traditions. Wellhausen's own judgment concerning the patriarchs is well-known: "It is true, we attain to no historical knowledge of the patriarchs, but only of the time when the stories about them arose in the Israelite people; this later age is here unconsciously projected . . . into hoary antiquity, and is reflected there like a glorified mirage."[2] For Wellhausen Israel's religion began with the Exodus; the patriarchs were but primitive nomads. The Israelite covenant was a late invention of the Deuteronomist in the seventh century. The distinction drawn between the priest and the Levite in connection with the tabernacle service was a post-Exilic idealization. Wellhausen and his followers dated the poetry of the Bible so late that the Psalms were assigned to the post-Exilic and even the Maccabean period.

At the beginning of the twentieth century a further development in literary criticism was the shift from the investigation of written "documents" to "form" criticism pioneered by Gunkel, who concentrated on the smaller genres or literary units. Recently Scandinavian scholars have laid great stress upon oral tradition. They would suggest that much of the biblical tradition was handed down orally before it was put down in writing at a later stage. We do know from the analysis of Homeric poems that traditions were faithfully transmitted by word of mouth for a period of 500 years from the time of the Trojan War until Homer *c.* 750 B.C.[3] Greece, however, experienced a Dark Age after the Dorian invasions of 1200 B.C. during which writing apparently disappeared. This is not true of Palestine where writing in different scripts is attested throughout the biblical periods.

In recent years the German scholars Albrecht Alt and Martin Noth have radically restructured Israelite history on the basis of literary criticism. Noth assumes an almost agnostic attitude about the patriarchs. They may have been historical but we cannot know anything definite about them. The Exodus and the Sinai traditions are completely separated; Moses was not the great founder of Israel's faith—"he arose out of a grave tradition at home in the steppes of Transjordan."[4] The story of a unified conquest of Palestine is viewed as unhistorical; instead the Israelites are said to have settled the land by a peaceful and gradual infiltration. Many of the stories in Joshua are nothing more than "aetiological" tales—"just-so" stories invented to explain some feature of the land, such as the twelve stones at Gilgal and the ruins of Ai. Radical interpretations such as these have been widely accepted since World War I. Speaking of the higher critical views developed by Wellhausen and successive scholars, John Bright notes:

> By the early decades of the twentieth century the virtual unanimity of scholarship in Europe and America had, in some cases with qualifications, been won over to it. It found embodiment in scores of histories, commentaries, introductions, and handbooks, many of which are still in use today. It is probable that thirty-five years ago few could have believed that it would ever be superseded.[5]

One of the striking characteristics of the scholars who have approached the Bible primarily through literary analysis is the non-use or at best the grudging use they have made of archaeological evidence. This is understandable for the nineteenth century and the early twentieth century when archaeology was in its infancy. Wellhausen, who was a great Arabic and Hebrew scholar, reconstructed Israelite life on the basis of Arabic poetry. He refused to believe that either Egyptian or Akkadian had been deciphered. On the other hand, Assyriologists since the 1890's and field archaeologists since the 1920's have discovered that their evidence accorded better with the biblical traditions than they did with Wellhausen's reconstructions.

A few scholars who had accepted the views of higher criticism, such as A. H. Sayce, reversed their positions because of the impact of the early archaeological discoveries, but most higher critics chose not to make use of the new data. "As late as 1932 a standard two-volume history of Israel appeared in print with scarcely a trace of having been influenced by the Amarna finds. Here then there has been a lag of about half a century."[6] The influential textbook, *Introduction to the Old Testament* (1941), by R. H. Pfeiffer of Harvard refers to the Ugaritic tablets only three times, though they had been deciphered over a decade before, and makes no mention of either the Lachish or the Samaria ostraca.

One of the contributing factors which prevented German Old Testament scholars from making greater use of archaeological data was the isolation imposed upon them by the political situation in the 1930's and 1940's.

> But after the middle 1930's Alt himself was cut off almost completely from direct contact with Palestine as well as from non-German research. His pupils (such as Martin Noth) were in much the same situation, and the attempt to replace the influx of empirical data from Palestine and the ancient Near East by systematic research along a priori lines led to increasing loss of touch with archaeological and philological fact. Today there is a very sharp cleavage between the dominant German school and the archaeological school, best represented in America and Israel.[7]

B. The Pre-Patriarchal Period

It is sometimes held that the early chapters of Genesis are but myths similar to Near Eastern creation accounts.[8] But an unprejudiced reading will disclose nothing that closely corresponds to the crassly anthropomorphic and polytheistic myths of Israel's contemporaries. It is true that it is possible to read between the lines and detect "demythologized" allusions, as some have done.

Late in the nineteenth century excavations at the famous library of Ashurbanipal in Nineveh turned up fragments of a Babylonian creation epic called *Enuma elish* "When above"— the first two words of the text. Gunkel has compared the Hebrew word *tehom* "the deep" in Gen. 1:2 with the Babylonian Tiamat, a primordial personification of sea water slain by Marduk. But the mere fact that the two words are related etymologically may simply stem from the fact that Hebrew and Akkadian are both Semitic languages with common roots; in meaning the two words are distinct. There is nothing in the Genesis account which even faintly resembles the crude mythology of *Enuma elish*, in which Marduk kills Tiamat and then cuts her open like a mussel shell to form the earth and the heavens.

Some scholars, such as Speiser and Orlinksy, have wished to translate Gen. 1:1 in a conditional sense, "When in the beginning . . . ," to make the verse correspond to the opening line of the Babylonian creation epic. This would radically change the sense of the initial verse of the Bible. The absolute rendering, "In the beginning . . .," yields the sense of an *ex nihilo* creation which is unique in the ancient world. It may be argued, however, that since the monotheism of the Hebrews is unique, it should hardly be surprising that their cosmogony is unique also. Until recently scholars had supposed that the Babylonian "Genesis" went back to the time of Hammurabi in the eighteenth century and predated the biblical Genesis. A study by Lambert has now dated this work to *c.* 1100 B.C., a period which would have been too late in any case to have influenced Moses.[9]

Another major Babylonian tale is the famous Gilgamesh Epic, the story of a king of Uruk (biblical Erech, modern Warka) who searched for immortality. Gilgamesh, who was considered partly divine in the legendary accounts, may now be regarded as a real king who reigned *c.* 2700 B.C. Following the initial publication of some of these Mesopotamian materials a group of German scholars, called by others the Pan-Babylonian School, attempted to explain practically everyone in the Bible in terms of their alleged Babylonian prototypes. Peter Jensen published three works from 1906 to 1926 in which he explained the figures of the patriarchs, the prophets, Jesus, and Paul as variants of the Gilgamesh image.

A sensation was created in 1872 by the publication of the eleventh Gilgamesh tablet, as it contained striking Babylonian parallels to the biblical flood story. George Smith, an erstwhile banknote engraver, made the exciting discovery while studying tablets in the British Museum. Some of the lines of the text were missing. A London newspaper, *The Daily Telegraph*, provided funds for George Smith to go to

3. Cuneiform tablet from Nineveh with Babylonian story of the flood. *(Courtesy, The British Museum.)*

Nineveh to find the missing portions. Hunting in the midst of hundreds of cuneiform tablets, Smith was, with incredible luck, able to find the missing pieces.

In 1929 in excavating Abraham's city of Ur in southern Mesopotamia, Leonard Woolley came upon a thick layer of water-borne sediment, eight to ten feet thick, which he claimed as evidence for *the* flood: "Taking into consideration all the facts, there could be no doubt that the flood of which we had thus found the only possible evidence was the Flood of Sumerian history and legend, the Flood on which is based the story of Noah."[10] Later study, however, has shown that there were other flood deposits at Kish, Fara, and Nineveh, which were not identical with the flood deposit at Ur, dated *c.* 4000 B.C. A recent study by Max Mallowan suggests that the flood of the Gilgamesh Epic should be identified with the flood deposit at Tell Fara (ancient Shuruppak, the home of Ziusudra—hero of the Sumerian story of the flood), and dated *c.* 2700 B.C.[11] One of the arguments for a date of 2700 B.C. would be the link with Gilgamesh who must have lived about this time. The flood episode, however, is not integrally bonded to the Gilgamesh story and may come from a much older period. The numerous flood stories, collected by James Frazer from the Near East, from Greece, from South Asia, from the Pacific, from the Americas, etc. seem to point to a deluge of an even greater antiquity. Albright has argued recently:

It is very difficult to separate a myth found all over the world, even as far away as pre-Columbian South America, from the tremendous floods which must have accompanied successive retreats of the glaciers in the closing phases of the Pleistocene Age. In other words, the Flood story presumably goes back, in one form or another, at least ten or twleve thousand years and, for all we know, much further.[12]

In 1965 the full text of an important Babylonian work including both a creation and a flood account—the Atrahasis Epic—was published. Before 1965 only one-fifth of the story had been known. The new tablets were discovered by Alan Millard stuffed away in a drawer of the British Museum. Whereas the *Enuma elish* traces the conflict between the older gods led by Tiamat and the younger gods led by Marduk to the boisterous behavior of the latter which kept their elders from sleeping, the new texts point to the refusal of the younger gods to continue their toil. It was in order to relieve the gods from labor that man was created. The flood was sent, according to the Atrahasis Epic, because men became too noisy for any of the gods to sleep. The overall plot of Creation—Rebellion—Flood found in the Atrahasis Epic is thus similar to the biblical story, though the ethical and theological contrasts are striking. On the question of whether or not there was borrowing, Millard concludes:

> In that the patriarch Abraham lived in Babylonia, it could be said that the stories were borrowed from there, but not that they were borrowed from any text now known to us. Granted that the Flood took place, knowledge of it must have survived to form the available accounts; while the Babylonians could only conceive of the event in their own polytheistic language, the Hebrews, or their ancestors, understood the action of God in it.[13]

Whereas in the Bible God sends the flood because of men's wickedness, the Babylonian gods send the flood because of their own annoyance at not being able to sleep. When the flood is over, Jehovah smells the sweet savor of Noah's sacrifice and blesses him (Gen. 8:21–9:1). When Utnapishtim, the hero of the Babylonian account, pours out a libation, "The gods smelled the sweet savor. The gods gathered like flies over the sacrificer," inasmuch as they had not received any nourishing sacrifices for a week.[14]

C. The Patriarchs

Until the breakthrough of archaeological discoveries, the stories about the biblical patriarchs—Abraham, Isaac, and Jacob—were subject to considerable skepticism. S. R. Driver explained the patriarchs as personifications of tribes. The Pan-Babylonian scholars H. Winckler and A. Jeremias interpreted them as reflections of astral deities. Others including Eduard Meyer and C. A. Simpson (in 1948!) regarded them as transformed Canaanite deities. Gunkel considered them as figures of folk poetry. More recently Noth and Eissfeldt concede that they were real persons but discount all the stories about them as unhistorical.

In the last thirty years, however, a steadily increasing flow of materials from Mesopotamia and Syria-Palestine—from Mari, from Nuzi, from Alalakh—has convinced all except a few holdovers, of the authenticity of the patriarchal narratives. Rowley points out that, "It is . . . not because scholars of today begin with more conservative presuppositions than their predecessors that they have a much greater respect for the patriarchal stories than was formerly common, but because the evidence warrants it."[15]

The exact date of the patriarchs is variously estimated by different scholars. The Bible in Ex. 12:40 speaks of the sojourn in Egypt, from the time of Jacob's entry to the Exodus, as lasting 430 years. The date of the entrance of Jacob into Egypt then depends on one's date of the Exodus. Conservative scholars who prefer a fifteenth century date for the Exodus place Abraham in the twenty-first century and Jacob's descent to Egypt in the nineteenth century. Many scholars, e.g. Albright, de Vaux, Yeivin, etc., on the basis of archaeological data have preferred the twentieth-nineteenth centuries B.C. for Abraham.

The over-all evidence would seem to indicate that the early

Middle Bronze Age fits in well with the background of the patriarchal narratives. Surveys by Glueck and Rothenberg in the Negeb and Sinai regions indicate seasonal occupation along caravan routes in the MB I (2000–1800 B.C.), and not for a millennium before or after. The picture of the patriarchs moving about in the hill country of Palestine fits in well with the population patterns of this time. They would have avoided the larger settlements of the coastal plains and the valleys in their search for pasturage for their flocks. The earlier migration of Abraham from Ur to Haran in northern Mesopotamia is also credible as both were great caravan cities as well as centers of the moon god Sin. Abraham's ancestors were idolaters (Josh. 24:2), and his father's name, Terah, may reflect an association with worship of the moon god.[16]

Many of the personal names of the patriarchal narratives have been found in the extrabiblical texts of the second millennium B.C. Similar to the name Abram is the name *Aba(m)rama* from Dilbat, and comparable to Abraham is the name *Aburahana* from the Egyptian execration texts. Similar to the name Terah is the name of *Turakhi*, a place near Haran. The name of Abraham's grandfather, Nahor (Gen. 11:25) is found in the name *Nakhur* at Mari. The name of Abraham's great grandfather, Serug is found in *Sharugi* near Haran. Names similar to Jacob have been found as in *Ya'qub-il* from Chagar-Bazar. The name of Laban has been found at Mari. Similar to Benjamin is the name *Binu-yamina* at Mari, meaning son of the right, i.e. south. It should be emphasized that none of these cases should be interpreted to mean that these refer to the actual biblical figures themselves, but in the words of Rowley, ". . . it is still valuable as evidence of verisimilitude in the biblical accounts, which use these names in that period."[17] Divine names which were rejected by a previous generation of scholars as fictional have also been found in the recent evidence.[18]

It will be noted that the evidence for the names of the patriarchal period come from the region around Haran and from Mari. Haran is in northwestern Mesopotamia; it was the city where Abraham and his father dwelt after leaving Ur (Gen. 11:31) on Abraham's way to Palestine. Haran has been subject to but limited soundings in the 1950's, and has not yet been systematically excavated.

Mari is on the middle section of the Euphrates River some 200 miles southeast of Haran. It may be that Abraham and his party passed through Mari from Ur to Haran. The site has been excavated by the French under André Parrot in more than fifteen seasons from 1933 to 1939 and then after World War II to the present. A royal palace covering twenty acres with 350 rooms, including a classroom, bathtubs and toilets, has emerged. Of the greatest importance are some 25,000 cuneiform (wedge-shaped writing) tablets from the royal archives. As Mari was destroyed by Hammurabi toward the end of the eighteenth century, the evidence from Mari comes from about the very same time as the patriarchs.

Another important site which has served to illuminate the patriarchal narratives is Nuzi in the Assyrian hill country. Edward Chiera excavated the site from 1925–31 for the American Schools of Oriental Research in Baghdad and Harvard University. The cuneiform tablets from Nuzi (c. 1500 B.C.) have cast much light on the social customs of the patriarchs.

Abraham's adoption of Eliezer of Damascus (Gen. 15:2) can be illustrated from the Nuzi texts, which show that it was the custom for childless couples to adopt a man as their heir. If later a son were born he would have to yield to the real son (Gen. 15:4). The incident in Gen. 16:1–2 which tells of Sarah presenting her handmaid Hagar to Abraham to beget a child is illustrated by a tablet of adoption which stipulates that a barren wife must provide a slave girl to her husband to beget a son. This particular tablet and the Hammurabi Law Code require that the slave's child be kept—a rule which was preempted by the divine command to send Hagar and Ishmael away. Esau's sale of his birthright to Jacob is paralleled in Nuzi by a man's transfer of his inheritance regarding a grove to his brother for three sheep.

Marriage customs in the patriarchal period are illumined by eighteenth century texts from Alalakh, a site in northern Syria on the Orontes River, excavated by Leonard Woolley in 1937–39 and in 1946–49. A husband who mistreated a wife (literally "drags her by the nose") had to give up his wife, her dowry, and the bridal gift which he had presented to her family. One text stipulates that a man may take a third wife only if his first two wives are barren. "Other contracts rule that if the wife 'fails to give birth in seven years he may take a second wife' (*The Alalakh Tablets* 93, 94). If this was in Jacob's first contract it might explain the need to wait a further seven years for Rachel (Gen. xxix. 18, 27)."[19]

One outstanding incident in the life of Abraham is the invasion of the four kings of the East—Amraphel, Arioch, Chedorlaomer, and Tidal—against the kings of Sodom and Gomorrah (Gen. 14). As noted in our introduction, Albright in an article written in 1918 regarded this chapter as unhistorical. Martin Noth in 1948 called it a late scholastic reconstruction. Nöldeke had earlier rejected it on the grounds that there was no route of march to the east of the Jordan River as described in the narrative. Such a route was found by Nelson Glueck, who reports:

Archaeological discovery has thus buttressed the accuracy of the biblical account of the existence and destruction of this long line of Middle Bronze I twenty-first–nineteenth century B.C.) cities by the kings of the East. Particularly remarkable and worthy of special emphasis is the fact that all of them were destroyed at the end of that period in the nineteenth century B.C., with only a few of them having ever again been reoccupied.[20]

Glueck suggests that the kings of the East were interested in the copper of the Arabah Valley south of the Dead Sea.

The Mari letters indicate that it was only in the period from c. 2000–1700 B.C. that the system of power alliances attested in Genesis 14 held true. The names of the eastern kings are foreign and have an authentic ring. Amraphel can no longer be identified with Hammurabi as was once popular, but the name accords well with several Amorite or Akkadian names. Arioch is similar to *Arriwuk*, a contemporary of Hammurabi. Speaking of *Arriwuk* Speiser maintains: "The form is comparatively rare, and not attested after the middle of the second millennium. Its appearance in the present context thus presupposes an ancient and authentic tradition."[21] The name Chedorlaomer contains tangible Elamite components (Elam was in southwestern Persia). Some scholars believe that Tidal represents the Hittite name *Tudkhaliya*. The word which is used for Abraham's armed retainers, *hanikim*, is found in the nineteenth–eighteenth century execration texts from Egypt. Speiser, who believes that Genesis 14 comes originally from a non-Israelite source, concludes that this passage is clear evidence that Abraham was a very real person and not a nebulous literary figure.[22]

Thus far we have dealt solely with areas where archaeological evidence has offered broad confirmation of the patriarchal narratives. We should also discuss areas where items of apparently late data crop up in what otherwise seem to be early materials. Such *anachronisms* occur especially in regard to ethnic and to geographic terms. I believe that it is necessary to distinguish between different kinds of anachronisms. An anachronism may have been an integral part of the original text and thus betray a serious misunderstanding on the part of the writer. On the other hand it is a universal practice for later editors or translators to make updated substitutions which are quite necessary to make certain items clear to later readers without elaborate circumlocutions.

It would be quite captious to place these deliberate substitutions in the same category and therefore under the same incriminating heading as erroneous anachronisms. In a strict sense it would be anachronistic to say, "The American Indians living in New Jersey in the fourteenth century belonged to the Piscataway tribe." We ought to say, "In the fourteenth century the redskinned aborigines (mistaken by Columbus as 'Indians') of the continent called 'America' (after the fifteenth century Italian explorer) living in the region which was later called 'New Jersey' (after the arrival of British colonists) belonged to the Piscataway tribe."

Similarly it is anachronistic in the strict sense to say, "The Jews living at Arad west of the Dead Sea guarded the southern approaches of Palestine in Hezekiah's time." The term "Jews" is derived from "Judeans" after the Babylonian Exile. The name "Dead Sea," *mare mortuum*, was brought into common use by Jerome or even coined by him.[23] The Old Testament name is *Yam ham-Melah* or "The Salt Sea." Palestine, which is derived originally from the Philistines, might be regarded as anachronistic if used of a period before the arrival of the latter. In actuality the Greek *Palaistine*, used by Herodotus in the fifth century B.C., and the Latin *Palaestina* did not become the official title of the country until the Romans replaced the distasteful name of *Judaea* after the revolt of A.D. 135.[24]

In the strict sense it would also be anachronistic for Egyptologists to speak of the Egyptian kings of the Old and Middle Kingdoms by the term "pharaoh" since this term which means literally "Great House" did not come into use for the king until the time of Akhnaton. It would also be anachronistic to speak of the Roman governors of Palestine before Pontius Pilate as "procurators"—although Tacitus does so—since the new Pilate inscription does not call him by this title. When we encounter such "harmless" anachronisms, we might better designate them as modernizations since they have been used for the benefit of later readers and do not affect the accuracy of the statements themselves. Albright has pointed out that:

> From the standpoint of the objective historian, data cannot be disproved by criticisms of the accidental literary framework in which they occur, unless there are solid independent reasons for rejecting the historicity of an appreciable number of other data found in the same framework.[25]

As our first example of an alleged anachronism we may take the mention of camels in the patriarchal narratives. In stressing his theory that Abraham was a "donkey caravaneer," Albright has repeatedly underscored the reference to camels in Genesis as anachronistic. He does concede that early nomads may have kept some camels before their successful domestication c. 1500–1250 B.C.[26] Eissfeldt[27] and Speiser, who consider the camel in the patriarchal stories as chronologically suspect, also leave open the possibility that camels may have come into limited use at an early date.[28]

On the other hand there are other scholars who find evidence, especially from art and from actual remains, for the domestication of camels in the patriarchal period. Parrot in 1961 came across camel bones in the center of Mari dating to c. 2500 B.C. and also a jar from the beginning of the second millennium on which the hindquarters of a camel are clearly recognizable.[29] Also from the early second millennium Kitchen cites a figurine from Byblos as well as Old Babylonian lexical texts and a Sumerian text from Nippur to demonstrate that Abraham and his descendants may very well have used camels.[30]

There are numerous problems connected with the various ethnic groups mentioned in Genesis. The famous Table of Nations (Gen. 10) would be dated to about the tenth century B.C. by Albright. The Madai of Gen. 10:2 are usually taken to be the Medes. The Medes and the related Persians make their first appearance in Assyrian texts of the ninth century B.C. On the basis of archaeological evidence scholars believe that new groups which can be associated with the Medes and the Persians entered the Iranian plateau about the tenth century B.C. A recent study by T. Cuyler Young, Jr., however, has argued on the basis of pottery that the Medes may have come into the area as early as the fourteenth century, so that we still need to keep our minds open to the possibility that some of the ethnic groups in the Table of Nations may have been on the scene even earlier than our present evidence indicates.

Another controversial issue concerns the "Hittites" or "children of Heth" in the Old Testament; in Hebrew the terms are respectively *hittî* and *benê het* (Gen. 15:20; 23:3). Excavations have shown that the Hittites were an Indo-European group who ruled an empire in Anatolia until *c.* 1200 B.C. On the one hand, Lehmann has called attention to what appear to be striking parallels between the Hittite Law Code and Abraham's transactions for the Cave of Machpelah with Ephron the "Hittite" in Genesis 23.[31] On the other hand, there is no evidence from the Hittite records themselves of any penetration of the Hittites south of Syria into Palestine, and very little archaeological evidence to support the claim that there were Hittites in this area. From the Late Bronze Age has come a cache of Hittite arms at Beth-shan, and from Megiddo a statuette of the god Resheph showing Hittite influence. Further evidence may perhaps turn up.

Some scholars such as Noth and Gurney view the term Hittite in the Old Testament as an anachronism used in its late Assyrian sense when the area of Syria-Palestine was known as "the land of Hatti." Hoffner has argued that the biblical *ḥittî* are an ethnic group that is unrelated to the Anatolian Hittites, and that the similarity in names is simply accidental.[32] A final suggestion is that of Speiser that the term may actually refer to the Hurrians inasmuch as the Septuagint (LXX) Greek translation and the Hebrew Masoretic Text (MT) confuse the Hurrians, Hittites, and Hivites more than once.

The Hurrians were a non-Semitic people originally from the area of Armenia, who were ruled by an Indo-European (Indo-Aryan) aristocracy of charioteers. They are the biblical Horites. There is also reason to believe that the biblical Jebusites and Hivites were also part of the Hurrian circle. There is no question but that the Hurrians did penetrate Syria and Palestine. The Amarna letters from Egypt give the name of the prince of Jerusalem in the fourteenth century as *Abdi-Kheba*, which means "The Slave of the Hurrian goddess Kheba." For the future temple David bought a threshing-floor from Araunah the Jebusite, a name which is related to the Hurrian *ewri* "lord."

The references to Aramaeans (translated "Syrians" in the KJV) in connection with the story of Laban have been regarded by some scholars as anachronistic. It is pointed out that the name of this Semitic group which spread eastward from Syria is attested only in the eleventh century B.C. A related nomadic tribe the *Akhlamu* are mentioned in the fourteenth century. De Vaux following Noth would regard the still earlier Amorites from Syria in the patriarchal period as "Proto-Aramaeans." Although some scholars would dispute the identification with the later Aramaeans, Dupont-Sommer has pointed out that the names "Aram" and

"Aramu" are already found at the end of the third millennium several centuries before the patriarchal age. [33] Parrot, who accepts the identification, says: "It is easy to recognize the *Aramu* of Mari as Aramaeans and this makes sense of the description 'Aramaean' which follows Laban's name (Gen. 25:20; 28:5; 31:20, 24), and also for the related liturgical formula from the Mosaic period—'A wandering Aramaean was my father'" (Deut. 26:5) [34] As as indication that Laban's designation as an Aramaean is not a later gloss is the fact that he is described as speaking Aramaic (Gen. 31:47).

On the other hand, the designation of Abraham's city of Ur in lower Mesopotamia as "Ur of the Chaldees" is readily explained as a gloss by a later editor as the Chaldaeans are nowhere mentioned in non-biblical texts until the eleventh century B.C.

As a final case we may consider the well-known anachronism of the reference to Philistines in the patriarchal stories. Holt, for example, says: "Perhaps it is wisest simply to admit that, if it is ever correct to speak of archaeological evidence as contradicting biblical material or as proving it anachronistic, the case of the Philistines in Genesis is one instance of it."[35] The first historical references to the Philistines are in the texts of Ramesses III (*c.* 1190 B.C.), though they are pictured in their typical "feather" or "horse-hair" headdresses in slightly earlier reliefs of the Sea Peoples who attacked Egypt. Some writers have held that the term "Philistine" in the narratives concerning Abimelech of Gerar (Gen. 20–21) may be intended to denote an earlier migration of people from the Aegean.[36] Amos 9:7 speaks of the Philistines as coming from Caphtor, which is usually interpreted as Crete, but perhaps by extension may designate the Aegean area influenced by the Minoan civilization of Crete.

Evidence for contacts between the Minoans and Mycenaeans of the Aegean and Palestine are multiplying with every excavation.[37] But most of the evidence, though it dates from before the twelfth century, does not reach back to the patriarchal period. An excavation at Tell Abu Hureira, which has recently been identified as Gerar—the city of Abimelech "the Philistine"—would help to clarify the issue. On the basis of the present evidence I would suggest that the term "Philistine" in the patriarchal narratives is a name which has been substituted for an earlier, no longer comprehensible term. Perhaps the basis of the substitution may have been the fact that Abimelech belonged to a stock which was indigenous to the area later dominated by the Philistines. It should be noted that all of the later references to the Philistines in the Old Testament accord well with the archaeological evidence.

D. In and Out of Egypt

As the scene of the action in the latter part of Genesis changes to Egypt with the story of Joseph, authentic Egyptian elements—including a number of Egyptian words—betray themselves.[38] In Gen. 41:1 the word for river, i.e. the Nile, is the Hebrew *ye'or*, derived from the Egyptian *'trw* or *'rw* before 1350 B.C. (The common girl's name "Susan" comes from Egyptian through Hebrew and means "lily.") There are a number of Egyptian names in the family of Joseph, and also in the Levitical family related to Moses and to Aaron. The Levitical names which are Egyptian are: Merari (Ex. 6:16) from *mrry* "beloved"; Pashhur (Jer. 20:1) from *psh Hr* "the portion of Horus"; Phinehas (I Sam. 1:3) from *pi-nehase* "the Nubian," which is an independent confirmation of the Nubian (Negroid Sudanese) element in the family of Moses (Num. 12:1).[39]

Joseph was not the first Semite sold into slavery in Egypt. The most important source on Semitic slaves in Egypt comes from 1740 B.C., about the time of Joseph.[40] This was one of the papyri bought by an American named Wilbour at the end of the nineteenth century but published only in 1953. It was only after Wilbour's death that his daughter presented the papyri, packed in cookie tins, to the Brooklyn Museum. This particular papyrus lists the names of almost a hundred slaves, about half of whom are designated "Asiatics," i.e. Semites from Palestine. Among the names are: *Mnhm*, cf. the name of the Israelite king Menahem; *'sh-ra*, cf. Asher; and *Shp-ra*, cf. Shiphrah, one of the midwives' names in Ex. 1:15—a name which Martin Noth had considered contrived. Incidentally the price of twenty shekels of silver paid for Joseph (Gen. 37:28) is the correct average price for slaves about the eighteenth century B.C. Due to inflation the price of slaves in the fifteenth century went up to thirty to forty shekels, and in the first millennium B.C. to fifty and even to one hundred shekels by Persian times. A shekel, which is about a quarter of an ounce, represented a month's average wage (e.g. in Hammurabi's Law Code).

Many other details of Egyptian background can be illustrated from both pictures and texts from Egypt.[41] Commenting on Genesis 41, which describes Joseph's elevation by the pharaoh, Speiser notes the following authentic details:

> Pharaoh elevates Joseph to the typically Egyptian post of Vizier (vs. 43). . . . The gift of the gold chain is another authentic touch. The three names in verse 45 are Egyptian in type and components; so, too, in all probability, is the escorts' cry "Abrek" (vs. 43).
>
> While the story is the main thing, the setting is thus demonstrably factual. And although the theme and the setting together cannot as yet be fitted into an established historical niche, the details are not out of keeping with that phase of Egyptian history which can be independently synchronized with the patriarchal period.[42]

Although the names in the Joseph narrative are genuinely Egyptian some of them are attested only in late Egyptian texts. This is the case with the name of Joseph's master *Potiphar* (Gen. 39:1); Joseph's wife *Asenath*, and Joseph's own new name *Zaphenath-Paneah* (Gen. 41:45), which are attested only from the twelfth century or even later in the tenth century. Montet, Kitchen, and Albright take this to mean that more modern substitutions were made during the transmission of the text. "Since almost exactly the same thing was done some seven centuries later by the Greek translators of Genesis (or by their Hebrew scribal source), the mere fact of such revision does not disprove the authenticity of the underlying tradition."[43] A more recent example is the substitution in our English translations of the New Testament of the name *James* (derived from the Spanish *Jaime*) for the Greek *Iakobos*, which is in turn a transliteration of the original Hebrew *Yacaqob* (English *Jacob*).

The apparent lack of early attestation in Egyptian sources for the names in the Joseph narrative may on the other hand be due to our almost complete lack of evidence for the Delta region where the story of Joseph takes place.[44]

The date of the Exodus is a problem which is linked with the date of the Conquest of Canaan some forty years later. Two dates have been proposed: an early date *c.* 1440 and a later date *c.* 1270. An inscription of the Egyptian pharaoh Merneptah mentions Israel in the land of Canaan by 1220, so the Exodus must have taken place at least forty years before this to allow for the time spent wandering in Sinai.

The arguments for the later date, which is that accepted by most scholars today, are as follows: 1) The surveys of Glueck in Transjordan show that the areas of Edom, Moab, and Ammon were lacking in settlements until the thirteenth century. The Bible indicates that the Israelites met opposition from settled populations in these areas. 2) The destruction of a number of Canaanite cities in the thirteenth century may plausibly be attributed to the Israelite invasion. 3) The mention of the city of Raamses (Ex. 1:11), built by the Hebrew slaves, is to be dated to the time of Ramesses II

(1304–1238 B.C.). This city has been identified with Tanis, excavated by Montet. Others would argue for the site of Qantir, fifteen miles south of Tanis. Both of these seem to have been original foundations by either Ramesses II or by his father Seti I.

American evangelical scholars such as Unger and Archer have defended the early date primarily on the basis of I Kings 6:1 which gives the chronological datum that Solomon began to build the temple 480 years after the Israelites came out of Egypt.[45] As Solomon built his temple about 960 B.C., adding 480 years would yield the date of 1440. To counter the arguments for a late date these scholars would, argue as follows: 1) They would point out that recent discoveries as at Amman have modified Glueck's original findings in the Transjordan.[46] 2) They would assign the thirteenth century

4. Pottery of the thirteenth century B.C. from Hazor. *Courtesy, The British Museum.*

destructions either to the Philistines or to the Judges and their enemies. 3) They would explain the reference to Raamses in Ex. 1:11 as a substitution of a later name for an earlier one.

The most attractive solution to the apparent contradiction between the datum of I Kings 6:1 and the archaeological evidence has been made by the British Egyptologist Kitchen. He suggests that the 480 years represents not simple elapsed time, but as in the case of some Egyptian records, the total of some years which may have been partly concurrent. The Turin Papyrus, for example, lists Dynasties XIII to XVII, whose total reigns amount to 450 years; but these pharaohs must have reigned partly concurrently within a 216 year period.[47] This mode of reckoning must also have been used for listing the separate years of the various Judges, whose lives must have overlapped in cases. This would compress the period of the Judges from a period of about four centuries (if the years listed were simply added together) to a period of two centuries.

German scholars such as Alt, von Rad, and Noth by using literary criticism have separated the Exodus tradition from the Sinai tradition on the supposition that these stories were the inheritance of different tribes. The two traditions were then combined artificially in the Twelve-Tribe League. Mendenhall's important study, however, has demonstrated that the Mosaic covenant follows the pattern of ancient Suzerainty treaties.[48] This means that the combination of the Mosaic covenant with the historical confession at Sinai is not an artificial device of a later editor but is a reflection of ancient literary patterns.[49] Mendenhall further demonstrates that the Sinai Covenant (Ex. 20; Josh. 24) is similar to the fourteenth-thirteenth century Hittite treaties, but differs from treaties of the first millennium.[50]

According to his preconceived notions, Wellhausen had held that Law had to follow Prophecy. This notion has been untenable since the discovery of the eighteenth century Code of Hammurabi in 1901 at Susa. For a half century this was

5. Ivory fragments from Ahab's Palace in Samaria. *Courtesy, The British Museum.*

our oldest known law code. Then in 1947 Francis Steele discovered a still earlier code—the nineteenth century Lipit-Ishtar Code—in, of all places, the basement of the University Museum in Philadelphia. These tablets had been unearthed at Nippur at the end of the nineteenth century A.D., but had lain unread on the museum shelves. The oldest law code of all is the twenty-first century Ur-Nammu Code, which was found in the Museum of the Ancient Orient in Istanbul. The text first came to the attention of Samuel N. Kramer in 1952.

Many of the so-called case laws (usually phrased "If . . ., then") in the Old Testament are similar to those found in these codes. A close parallel may be seen in the laws of "the goring ox." Ex. 21:35 reads: "And if one man's ox hurt another's, that he die; then they shall sell the live ox, and divide the money of it; and the dead ox also they shall divide." Paragraph fifty-three of the nineteenth century Laws of Eshnunna is almost identical: "If an ox gored an ox and caused (it) to die, both ox owners shall divide the price of the live ox and the carcass of the dead ox."[51]

There are differences between the case laws of the Hebrews and the Mesopotamians. These differences reflect a higher regard for human life manifested among the Hebrews.[52] For example, according to the Code of Hammurabi a Babylonian master could kill his own slave with impunity since he was considered to be a piece of property. A Hebrew master who killed his own slave would have been tried for murder. Albrecht Alt has drawn the distinction between "casuistic" or case laws, and "apodictic" law as exemplified in the direct commands of the Ten Commandments. Strictly speaking apodictic formulae are to be found in the declaratory statements of the Hammurabi Code, in the terse commands in the Laws of Eshnunna, and in interdictions in funerary inscriptions. But these are not true parallels to the broad ethical injunctions of the Decalogue, which appear to be unique.

Interesting evidence, though it is negative evidence, appears from the excavations which may relate to the observation of the second commandment's prohibition of idols. Wright observes:

> But the fact remains that whereas male idols occur in nearly every excavation in known Canaanite ruins, only one to my knowledge has ever been unearthed in the vast amount of debris moved by

6. Pictorial representation: The tribute of Jehu, the king of Israel, Before Shalmaneser III of Assyria. *Courtesy, The British Museum.*

excavators from Israelite towns. This fact has to be reckoned with. . . . While male images may turn up, the evidence is already overwhelming that they were exceedingly rare.[53]

E. The Conquest of The Promised Land

The date of the Conquest is closely tied up with the date of the Exodus as discussed above. Among the arguments used by the advocates of the earlier date of 1440 for the Exodus is the possible association of the biblical Hebrews with the Habiru of the fourteenth century Amarna letters from Egypt.[54] It is clear that the Habiru were widespread from the many notices of them in the seeond millennium. The earliest references to the Habiru are in texts from the nineteenth century from Alishar in central Turkey. In the eighteenth—seventeenth centuries they are mentioned at Alalakh, Haran, and Mari. In the fifteenth century they appear in Egypt, where they are called Apiru, and in the fourteenth century in Palestine. Most scholars follow Landsberger in thinking of the Habiru as composed of diverse ethnic elements, and having in common only a generally inferior social status.[55] Albright, who believes that the word "Apiru" can be interpreted as "dusty one"—that is, a donkey caravaneer—believes that this can be used to explain the background of Abraham. De Vaux and Parrot also believe that the Hebrews may have been part of the broader movement of the Habiru. They would not, however, agree that this association could be used as evidence for an early date of the Exodus and Conquest.

The prevailing higher critical view of the Conquest is based on contrasting the stories of Joshua with that of Judges 1. According to this view Joshua depicts the Conquest as due to a full-scale national war, whereas Judges depicts a more piecemeal campaign or even long scale peaceful infiltration. Literary critics have supposed that the latter account was earlier, whereas the former was a late "epic of conquest."[56] Kaufmann has argued that these stories are not late inventions but accurate descriptions of the strategy of conquest.[57] Excavations seem to have proved him right.

Archaeologists have found signs of the widespread destruction of Canaanite cities in the thirteenth century. Not all of these destructions can be certainly attributed to the Israelites as the Philistines who arrived late in the thirteenth

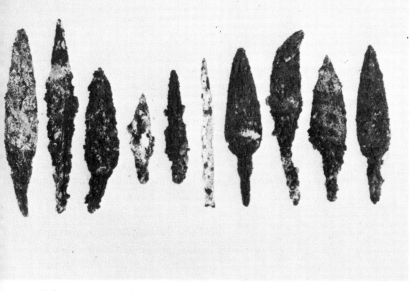

7. Bronze, bone, and iron arowheads from the siege of Lachish. *Courtesy, The British Museum.*

century may have been responsible for the destruction of sites close to the coast. Signs of destruction at Tell el-Hesi (Eglon?) may be attributed either to the Israelites or to the Philistines. The burning of Lachish may even be due to a campaign by pharaoh Merneptah. A bowl inscribed in Egyptian, probably dating from Merneptah's reign, was found in the destruction level at Lachish.[58] The destruction of Ashdod on the Philistine coast is probably to be attributed to the Philistines, although the excavator, Moshe Dothan, has suggested that it may have been due to the Israelites.[59] It is certain that the Philistines destroyed Ashkelon since Philistine pottery appears above the layer of ash.

Unambiguous evidence for Joshua's campaign comes from the excavations of Yigael Yadin at Hazor, fifteen miles north of the Sea of Galilee. Hazor was the largest city in Palestine in the Late Bronze Age (Josh. 11:10), sustaining a population of some 40,000. The site of Hazor is comprised of an upper city of thirty acres and a lower plateau of 175 acres. The lower plateau was defended by great earthen embankments together with a dry moat. The rampart at the top of the moat would have been almost a hundred feet above the bottom of the moat—a seemingly impregnable fortress! Yet it was taken and burned by Joshua (Josh. 11:1–13).[60]

Evidence for Joshua's southern campaign may be seen in the four feet of "black and ash-filled earth, fallen brick now burned red, and charred and splintered debris" found at Bethel, a few miles north of Jerusalem. The excavator, James Kelso comments:

We have never seen indications of a more destructive conflagration in any other Palestinian excavation, a fact which suggests extensive use of wood in Iron I construction at Bethel. The cultural break between LB (Late Bronze) and Iron I was also more complete than in any other similar break at Bethel . . . . We are compelled to identify it with the Israelite conquest.[61]

Even farther to the south at Tell Beit Mirsim, which Albright has identified as Debir (Josh. 15:16 ff.), evidence for a thirteenth century conflagration was recovered.

The archaeological evidence also seems to support the biblical record in respect to cities that were not captured and destroyed. Egyptian strongholds in Canaan were not taken by the Israelites. Kelso observes:

> To appreciate the complete cultural and religious change brought by the Israelites one need only turn to such cities as Megiddo, Taanach, and Beth-shean, which were not captured by Joshua (Josh. 17:11–12). The excavations of these cities show a Canaanite culture and cult continuing unchanged by Joshua's conquest.[62]

The biblical record which indicates that Shechem passed peacefully into Israelite control, probably by treaty, is in accord with the archaeological evidence. According to Ross:

> The peaceful passage of Shechem from Canaanite to Israelite control is an important historical datum. The absence of the city from lists of Joshua's conquests and its importance as a center for early Israelite tribal life have been interpreted as indicating that Shechem was in friendly hands when the Israelites entered Palestine. The archaeological data lend considerable support to this theory.[63]

Along with the positive evidence presented here for a thirteenth-century Conquest, there are three sites which present apparently contradictory evidence or at least a lack of evidence for this reconstruction: Jericho, Gibeon, and Ai. At Jericho the earlier excavations in 1930–36 by John Garstang had uncovered walls which the excavator identified as those of Joshua's city *c.* 1400 B.C. Kenyon's recent excavations in 1952–58 have shown that Garstang's walls are in fact remains from the Early Bronze Age, a thousand years before Joshua's time. Kenyon's work uncovered no Late Bronze (1500–1200 B.C.) walls. The only buildings that can be attributed to this period are foundations of a single wall with about a square meter of intact floor and a so-called "Middle Building" uncovered by Garstang. Of over a thousand tombs less than ten can be attributed to the Late Bronze Age.[64] From the limited evidence Kenyon suggests that the latest Bronze Age occupation should be dated *c.* 1325, which accords neither with the early nor with the late date proposed for the Conquest.

How shall we explain this apparent lack of concord between the biblical record and the archaeological evidence? Several suggestions have been made: 1) Noth and Gray suggest that the story in Joshua is an aetiological tale, that is, a popular story devised to explain some of the earlier fallen walls. 2) Kenyon considers the possibility that the earlier Middle Bronze Age walls might have been re-used: "The Late Bronze Age town must either have re-used this, or a new wall may have been built above it, so nothing remains of it."[65] There is, however, no evidence of such re-use at the small portion of Middle Bronze rampart which has been uncovered. 3) A fact which must certainly be taken into consideration is the extraordinary degree of erosion which has taken place at Jericho. Over most of the summit of the tell even the houses of the populous Middle Bronze Age town have vanished. Kenyon concedes: "It must be admitted that it is not impossible that a yet later (than 1325 B.C.) Late Bronze Age town may have been even more completely washed away than that which so meagerly survives."[66] 4) The final possibility which I would suggest is that since the excavations by Sellin, Garstang, and Kenyon have not exhausted the eight-acre site, future excavations may still unearth the missing Late Bronze remains. Paul Lapp notes that:

Even Jericho, one of the most fully excavated sites in Palestine, could still keep a large expedition busy for many years. In fact, Miss Kenyon has planned her excavations so that substantial portions of the tell will remain available for future excavations when archaeological methodology has been improved and new techniques and analyses developed and refined.[67]

A similar problem surrounds the lack of much Late Bronze materials from Gibeon, excavated for five seasons by James B. Pritchard between 1956–63. In the first three seasons nothing of the Late Bronze period was found. In the areas excavated on the tell no building remains and only a few potsherds of this period were found. Then in 1960 the excavators found two richly furnished tombs of the Late Bronze period. When the contents of all the tombs were restudied five more Late Bronze burial deposits were noted. As to the implications of these finds, Pritchard has said: "The Late Bronze tombs of the fourteenth century belonged either to a very small settlement, limited to some small section of the mound as yet untouched, or to the temporary camps in the vicinity. There can be no doubt, on the basis of the best evidence available, that there was no city of any importance at the time of Joshua."[68]

In another article Pritchard expressed himself more cautiously as follows:

The history of the biblical city of Gibeon, although better known than it was when we first began excavation, is far from complete. Much of the evidence has been irretrievably denuded from the top of the wind-swept hill on which the city stood, and much of it remains to be uncovered in land that, for the present at least, is under cultivation in the olive orchards and vineyards of the peasants who eke out a livelihood in the village of el-Jib.[69]

Rainey has also suggested the possibility that the Late Bronze remains may have been eroded from Gibeon. He writes, "I suspect that there may have been a settlement of some kind of which no remains were uncovered; all hill country sites have suffered a great deal through the ages and bedrock is usually not far from the surface, especially at the top of the mound."[70] Again as in the case of Jericho it is quite possible that five seasons of excavations which reached bedrock in six areas have not yet uncovered all there is to know about the sixteen-acre site. Kenyon, commenting upon the relatively scanty Late Bronze materials from the tombs at Gibeon remarks: "The existence of even this small amount of material makes it likely that there was a town there at this period, and that the Late Bronze Age cemetery was outside the comparatively small area excavated."[71]

The third problem site is that of biblical Ai, usually identified with et-Tell about two miles east of Beitin (Bethel). Excavations at et-Tell by Mme. Judith Marquet-Krause and S. Yeivin from 1933–35 showed that there was a complete break in occupation from 2000–1200 B.C. Recently four seasons of work at et-Tell were conducted under Joseph A. Callaway from 1964 until 1969. The latest results have confirmed the lack of occupation in the Middle and Late Bronze periods.

Because of the puzzling lack of Late Bronze materials to correspond with the city taken by Joshua various alternative sites have been proposed, and other solutions suggested: 1) It has been suggested that Ai should be located at another site since no epigraphic evidence has positively identified et-Tell as Ai. But recent soundings at the alternative sites of Khirbet Khudriya, Khirbet Haiyan, and Khirbet Hai have not turned up any Late Bronze materials. 2) A second solution is that of Martin Noth, who explains the biblical story as an etiological tale devised to explain "ruins" found at the site by Israelites, as the name "Ai" in Hebrew means a "heap of stones." 3) L. H. Vincent suggested that the people of Bethel temporarily erected a military outpost on the ruins called Ai. 4) Albright supposes that the conquest of Ai actually reflects the capture of Bethel, and suggests that the names of the two sites were confused by later editors. 5) The excavator Callaway has recently proposed a radical reinterpretation.[72] He would interpret the thirteenth century destructions at Bethel, Hazor, etc. as the work of pre-Israelite invaders, and would argue that the Israelite invasion actually took place in the Iron Age early in the twelfth century. To support this view he cites the lack of Late Bronze materials at Gibeon and at Arad.[73] 6) Finally I would suggest that the Late Bronze materials may still lie hidden in the twenty-seven-acre mound, especially as the large northeastern area appears not to have been sounded.[74] If, however, the areas excavated are representative of the site's complete occupational history—as

8. Inscribed ostracon from Lachish. *Courtesy, The British Museum.*

we must for the present assume—the problem of Ai remains a very serious and unresolved enigma.[75]

In summarizing the problems of these three Conquest sites, Paul Lapp has expressed an optimistic viewpoint: "The problems are not insurmountable: evidence of conquest occupation may have eroded away at Jericho; Bethel may have been 'the ruin' that was Ai of the conquest account, and the Late Bronze town may still be awaiting the excavator's spade at Gibeon."[76] Lapp, who is otherwise exceedingly cautious in claiming the confirmation of a biblical narrative on the basis of archaeological evidence is convinced that the best explanation of the series of thirteenth century destructions is the biblical account of Joshua's campaign. He asks: "It is possible to attribute these destructions to Egyptian campaigns, Sea Peoples without their characteristic pottery, or internecine struggles, but why promote such postulations in the face of clear statements in the biblical sources that these two sites (Hazor and Lachish) were destroyed by Joshua."[77]

After the destructions of the thirteenth century we have evidence which may surely be interpreted as belonging to the Israelite settlements. Well-built Canaanite houses are replaced by cruder buildings. Beebe remarks, "Usually the Israelite owner used more energy with poorer results than the occupant before him."[78] Some of these new settlements follow very shortly after the destruction levels, as at Bethel. Albright notes that: "This means that the Israelite invasion was not a characteristic irruption of nomads, who continued to live in tents for generations after their first invasion. Neither was the Israelite conquest of Canaan a gradual infiltration, as is often insisted by modern scholars."[79] Uniform pottery over a dozen sites including et-Tell, Tell en-Nasbeh, Shiloh, Beth-zur, and Tell el-Ful testify to the settlement of Israelites at these sites during the end of the thirteenth or the beginning of the twelfth centuries. It is also noteworthy that after 1220 B.C. Canaanite temples are no longer built at such cities. At Bethel the re-use of a sacred Canaanite pillar as an ordinary building stone shows that the Israelites had no superstitious dread of the pagan cult object.[80]

For the subsequent period archaeology has confirmed the general picture of chaos depicted in the book of Judges during the twelfth–eleventh centuries when the Israelites were consolidating their hold on captured areas. Wright points out that:

> Every town thus far excavated was destroyed from one to four times, at least, during these two centuries. Yet so far few of the destructions can be correlated with one another; and this suggests precisely what the Book of Judges implies: namely, that the fighting was continuous and largely local in nature.[81]

The evidence from Shechem shows that there was a destruction there *c.* 1150–1100 B.C. which may be linked with the story of Shechem's destruction by Abimelech, Gideon's son (Judges 9). Wright believes that the temple of El-Berith mentioned in the story is the same as a temple uncovered by his excavations.[82]

One of the most celebrated victories of the Judges is that of Deborah and Barak over Sisera recorded in Judges 4–5. Excavations indicate that both Megiddo and Taanach suffered a major destruction at 1125 B.C., the probable date of Deborah's victory. As the tribe of Manasseh had not succeeded in driving out the Canaanites of Taanach and Megiddo during the Conquest (Judges 1:27), it is probable that the populations of these cities joined Sisera in fighting the Israelites. The Israelite triumph over the Canaanite chariots was achieved because providential rains swelled the little Kishon Brook and made the Esdraelon Plain a quagmire

(Judges 5:21). It is interesting to note that Sellin while excavating Taanach reported that the spring rains made travel difficult for his wagons. In 1903 three of his horses drowned in the swollen Kishon.

F. Saul, David, and Solomon

On the heels of the Israelite invasion of Canaan from the east came the invasion of the Philistines and other Sea Peoples from the west. Archaeological evidence has shown that the Philistines reached the peak of their power in the early eleventh century before the accession of Saul as Israel's first king—which harmonizes with the biblical account of this period. The Philistines were in conflict with the Israelites in the period of the Judges, and of Saul and David.

The most important evidence for Saul's reign comes from the excavation of Tell el-Ful just north of Jerusalem. It is a site which commands a spectacular view and was chosen as the location of a new palace for King Hussein of Jordan. Tell el-Ful is probably the site of Saul's capital of Gibeah. The fortress excavated by Albright reveals the simplicity of Saul's court. The building itself was probably built originally by the Philistines (I Sam. 10:5) and re-used by Saul. Among the objects found were bronze arrowheads, sling stones, and an iron plow point. The Philistines had been able to maintain military superiority at first by monopolizing the new technology of manufacturing iron implements (I Sam. 13:19–22). The Philistines defeated Saul at the battle of Gilboa and hung his body in the temple of Dagon at Beth-shan. After rescuing the corpses of Saul and his sons, the men of Jabesh-Gilead cremated their bodies (I Sam. 31:12–13), an unusual practice which may have been introduced into the area from the Aegean by the Philistines.

The contest between David and Goliath reveals a number of interesting parallels with Homeric warfare as befits the

Aegean origin of the Philistines. The name Goliath, Hebrew *Golyat*, has been compared to the Lydian *Alyattes*. (Lydia was located in western Asia Minor.)[83] Goliath had on a helmet of bronze similar no doubt to those worn by the Homeric heroes. He is said to have worn greaves (shin-guards) of bronze (I Sam. 17:6). "Well-greaved" is the most frequent epithet of the Achaeans in Homer. The wearing of greaves was a distinctive feature of warriors from an Aegean background.[84]

After David's victory over Goliath and his temporary stay at the king's court, he had to assume the role of a fugitive because of Saul's intense jealousy. An inscribed javelin head from El-Khadr between Bethlehem and Hebron has been interpreted by Mazar as perhaps belonging to a soldier attached to the forces of David during his exile from the court. At one point in his flight David had the opportunity to slay Saul as he was sleeping in a cave, but instead cut off the hem of Saul's garment (I Sam. 24:4). The real significance of this act may be seen from texts found at Alalakh and Mari. Wiseman explains: "Another symbolic act here (at Alalakh), as at Mari, is 'to seize (or let go) the hem of the garment' which denotes the giving of unreserved submission to (or defection from) a person . . ., which may imply that David's act in cutting off the 'wing' or hem of Saul's garment was an act of rebellion for which he was later repentant . . . ."[85]

Although the Psalms are not all ascribed to David and although the very superscriptions may be of late date (as indicated by the variations in the Cave XI Psalms Scroll from Qumran), it may be convenient to comment here on the bearing of recent finds on the dating of the Psalms. Critical scholars following the lead of Wellhausen and Duhm dated the Psalms to the post-Exilic period because their level of religion seemed too advanced for an earlier age. R. H. Pfeiffer dated the great majority of the Psalms between 400 and 100 B.C. in his introduction to the Old Testament published in 1941. The discoveries at Ugarit on the one hand and at Qumran on the other have shown that the Psalms are to be dated early rather than late in Israel's history. Many scholars have shown that the Ugaritic texts yield exact parallels to the poetic patterns and verbal combinations of the Psalms, Proverbs, and other biblical texts. As Ugarit was destroyed c. 1200 B.C. these parallels imply an early date. Albright comments: "Actually much early Hebrew verse dates from the second millennium, and was composed in a poetic dialect closely related to the generalized epic dialect of Canaan in which Ugaritic verse was composed."[86]

These conclusions for the early dating of the Psalms have not been accepted by some scholars who still wish to maintain their late date. Morton Smith argues that Ugaritic traditions probably lived on in Phoenician cities and may have been absorbed by the Jews in the Persian period. Smith reasons as follows:

But we know from Philo of Byblos that traditions like the Ugaritic lived on in Phoenician cities down to Roman times, and Phoenician contacts with the Israelites were particularly close towards the end of the Persian period . . . . Relations continued close in the hellenistic age, as we know from remains of the "Sidonians" at Marisa; and there is nothing unlikely in the notion that the Jerusalem priesthood of these periods, which was in close and friendly contact with the neighboring peoples, may have been responsible for the introduction of Phoenician elements into the temple psalms.[87]

But the so-called "Phoenician" elements in the Psalms are not attenuated traditions such as those handed down in the Greek text of Philo of Byblos, accurate in outline though these may be, but rather verbal correspondences to Ugaritic in matters of literary style. That this was a heritage from the Canaanites passed on to the Davidic musical guilds seems to be a much more likely explanation for such parallels than hypothetical borrowings from Phoenician sources in the Hellenistic age.

The new evidence from Qumran gives us many original Hebrew compositions of the Hellenistic age. With the exception of the non-canonical additions to the Cave XI Psalms Scroll, the Qumran compositions do not resemble the Psalter. The Thanksgiving Hymns of the Dead Sea community are largely made up of mosaics of biblical quotations. In the light of the new materials from Ugarit and from Qumran, Albright offers the following conclusion as to the date of the Psalms:

> There can be little doubt, in my opinion, that there are scores of Psalms whose composition may best be dated in the tenth century or shortly afterwards, and it becomes hypercritical to reject the tradition of Davidic sponsorship (which was tantamount to authorship at that early period) of a substantial nucleus of the present Book of Psalms. [88]

Solomon as a wealthy and energetic king has left many evidences of his building activities behind him. Unfortunately very little if anything from Jerusalem can be attributed to him. The recent excavations by Kenyon in Jerusalem have revealed a few structures in the northern part of the Ophel ridge which may possibly be Solomonic or a little later: a casemate wall, some well-cut blocks similar to those cut by Phoenician masons at Samaria, and a proto-Ionic capital. The so-called "Millo" or "filling" (I Kings 9:15, 24) which was rebuilt by David and Solomon is considered by Kenyon to be the terraces of the slopes of Ophel which needed constant repair.

When Solomon had finished his temple at Jerusalem he gave a great feast (I Kings 8:65). An interesting ninth century Assyrian parallel has come to light in the stele of Ashurnasirpal II found at Nimrud. The king boasted: "The happy people of all the lands together with the people of Kalhu

(Nimrud), for ten days I feasted, wined, bathed, anointed and honoured them and then sent them back to their lands in peace and joy.[89] Believe it or not, there were 69,574 party guests!

At Megiddo the remains of stables consisting of stalls with perforated stone pillars for tethering horses and limestone mangers have long been known as "Solomon's" stables. Upon re-examination of the site by Yadin in 1960, these structures have turned out to be from the later period of Ahab's reign. As a matter of fact the biblical text (I Kings 9:15-19) does not explicitly mention stables at Megiddo. It may still be, however, that Solomonic structures may lie under the pavement of Ahab's stables which have been left *in situ.*

While digging at the Solomonic level at Hazor, Yadin had a brilliant inspiration. Basing his hunch on the biblical statement that Solomon had built "Hazor, and Megiddo, and Gezer" (I Kings 9:15), he recalled the fact that the Megiddo excavation had found a Solomonic gate with three chambers on each side.

Before proceeding further with the excavation, we made tentative markings of the ground following our estimate of the plan of the gate on the basis of the Megiddo gate. And then we told the laborers to go ahead and continue removing the debris. When they had finished, they looked at us with astonishment, as if we were magicians or fortune-tellers. For there, before us, was the gate whose outline we had marked, a replica of the Megiddo gate. This proved not only that both gates had been built by Solomon but that both had followed a single master plan.[90]

A re-examination of Macalister's report on Gezer revealed that half of an identical Solomonic gate had unwittingly been excavated there also.

Among the activities for which Solomon is noted is his work of mining copper. The recent work by Pritchard at Tell esSa'idiyeh east of the Jordan River has uncovered a large number of bronze objects from the pre-Solomonic period. Pritchard and Glueck would identify this large mound with biblical Zarethan, a bronze-working center in the days of Solomon (I Kings 7:45–46). It was particularly the labors of Nelson Glueck which have revealed to us the existence of numerous copper mines in the Arabah Valley south of the Dead Sea and the Solomonic port of Eziongeber at Tell el-Kheleifeh on the Red Sea. Additional sites have been discovered by Beno Rothenberg, who has shown that the copperbearing ores were smelted in open pits on charcoal fires fanned by bellows. At Tell el-Kheleifeh relatively little slag was found. Glueck explains that this is a result of the re-smelting in pottery smelters of already refined copper globules. The ancient miners extracted the metal from lumps of copper sulphide, containing forty to forty-five percent copper. The modern Israeli Timnah Copper Works are able to extract the metal from chrysocolla ore which contains only two percent copper.[91] A building with holes in its walls at Tell el-Kheleifeh was originally interpreted by Glueck as a smelter or foundry with flue holes. Accepting the criticisms of Rothenberg, Glueck now considers the building to have been simply a storehouse or granary.[92]

Glueck's original discovery of the site of Tell el-Kheleifeh was inspired by strict attention to the biblical text. "The whereabouts of Solomon's long-lost port city of Ezion-geber was for centuries an unfathomable mystery, because no one paid attention to the biblical statement that it was located 'beside Eloth, on the shore of the Red Sea, in the land of Edom' (I Kings 9:26; 10:22). And that is exactly where we found it . . . ."[93] The site is today located just on the Jordanian side of the Jordan-Israeli boundary.

The passage in II Chron. 8:17–18 informs us that in conjunction with Phoenician sailors sent to him by Hiram of Tyre, Solomon sent out expeditions to bring back gold from

Ophir. That this was not a legendary land is shown by the discovery of an eighth century ostracon with the text, "gold of Ophir for Beth Horon, thirty shekels," found at Tell Kasile just north of Tel Aviv. The location of Ophir has been variously placed in Arabia, on the Somali coast of Africa, and in India. In favor of a possible identification of Ophir with (S)upara, a port sixty miles north of Bombay, is the interpretation of the Septuagint and of Jerome, and also the nature of the products brought back from the expeditions (I Kings 10:22–24; II Chron. 9:10–11, 21–22). Barnett suggests that the words in the Hebrew original for sandalwood, peacock, and ape (Hebrew *almug* or *algum*, *tukki*, and *kof*) are related to the Indian words *agil*, *tokei*, and *kapi*.[94]

The ships of Tarshish which Solomon used in his expeditions were ocean-going vessels. The name Tarshish means a smelter, and there were a number of sites with this name. The most famous was distant Tartessus, a Phoenician outpost in southern Spain. Although most classical scholars have dated the Phoenician expansion to the west only to the eighth century B.C., Albright on the basis of new evidence dates this activity to the time of Solomon. "By the middle of Hiram I's reign, about 950 B.C., we may suppose that Gades (Cadiz) and Tartessus had been founded."[95]

Solomon's trade with another region has been obscured by a mistranslation in the King James Version. In I Kings 10:28 the word translated "linen yarn" actually means "from Cilicia"—the region in southeast Turkey where the best horses were to be obtained. The verse should therefore read: "And Solomon's horses were exported from Cilicia."[96]

We are informed in I Kings 9:16 that an unnamed Egyptian king went up to Palestine, took Gezer, and gave it to Solomon along with the hand of his daughter. A. Malamat has suggested that Siamun, a king of the XXI Dynasty, invaded Palestine soon after the death of David to put the new king to the test. There is evidence of destruction at Tel Mor (the port of Ashdod), at Beth-shemesh, and at Gezer, which may possibly be attributed to this raid. Since we know from the Amarna Letters that the Egyptians condescended to marry foreign princesses but as a rule disdained to give their own princesses in marriage, it is an indication of Solomon's power and prestige and also of Egypt's weakness that he was able to obtain territory from and arrange a diplomatic marriage with Egypt.

Solomon's successor Rehoboam did not fare as well at the hand of the Egyptians. We are informed that in his fifth year Shishak came up against Jerusalem and took away the treasures of the temple (I Kings 14:25–26). We learn from Shishak's own reliefs and texts at Karnak that he conquered not only Judah but cities in the Esdraelon Valley, Trans-jordan, and Edom as well. A monumental stele of Shishak has been found at Megiddo to confirm his claim.

G. The Divided Kingdoms

The financially exhausting policy of Solomon and of his son Rehoboam led to the revolt of the ten northern tribes under Jeroboam I, who set up the northern kingdom of Israel with centers of worship at Bethel and at Dan. The excavators of Bethel searched in vain for the site of Jeroboam's shrine, which still remains hidden in the unexcavated portion of Beitin. Since 1966 A. Biran has been excavating at the northern site of Dan. Until the 1967 war the site served as the northernmost outpost of Israel close to the borders of Leba-non and Syria. Biran has discovered a monumental city gate built by Jeroboam I, the largest ever discovered in Palestine.

The sixth king of Israel was a usurper named Omri (876–69 B.C.), who attacked Zimri at his capital of Tirzah. Excavations by R. de Vaux at Tell el-Farah, which has been identified as Tirzah, have revealed a burnt level which may be the result of Omri's attack. Omri resided at Tirzah for six years before building a new capital at Samaria (I Kings 16:23). Unfinished construction at Tell el-Farah seems to belong to the city which Omri abandoned. The new capital at Samaria reveals fine Phoenician masonry from the time of Omri and his son Ahab. Commenting on the implications of the buildings for the relationship of the king to his people, Franken notes:

> The king was no longer chosen by the tribes as in the days of Saul. Omri, himself a usurper of the throne, knew the dangers that threatened his dynasty, not only from foreign powers like Damascus but also from court intrigues and ambitious military men. It also shows us that the king was no longer content to live a simple life as father of his people, but desired to bring his court in line with contemporary ruling powers, and live in some style and luxury, segregated from the mass of his people.[97]

Ahab (869–50 B.C.) married the notorious Jezebel, a Phoenician princess, which explains the presence of Phoenician masonry at Samaria. Ahab's "ivory house" (I Kings 22:39) has been illustrated by many pieces of ivory found at Samaria from the ninth–eighth century levels. From nonbiblical texts we learn that Ahab was not only a wealthy but also a powerful king. The Bible does not mention the battle of Qarqar in Syria in 853 B.C., but the texts of Shalmaneser III of Assyria indicate that Ahab joined various kings against the Assyrians and that he supplied 2,000 chariots and 10,000 men. The power of Omri and of Ahab earned the respect of the Assyrians, who referred to Israel as *bit-Humri* ("the House of Omri"), and to her kings as *mar-Humri* ("the son of Omri"), long after the dynasty had disappeared.

A fascinating light is shed on the activities of Omri and his successors in Transjordan by the famous Moabite Stone of Mesha, king of Moab. The Bible does not mention it but the Moabite Stone reveals that it was Omri who conquered

Moab, the area east of the Dead Sea. According to the Moabite version this defeat resulted from the anger of the god Chemosh with his own people. The text goes on to say: "And Omri had taken possession of the land of Medeba and (Israel) dwelt in it his days and half the days of his son, forty years."[98] If the "son" of Omri should be taken to be Ahab there would be a discrepancy with the biblical account (II Kings 3:5) which indicates that the Moabite revolt took place after Ahab's death. "If, however, the word be interpreted as 'grandson' (as is frequent in the Bible), then the historical problem is solved and the round number 'forty years' becomes intelligible."[99] The Bible does say that in the days of Omri's grandson a joint expedition led by Joram and by Jehoshaphat of Judah attacked Moab but apparently suffered defeat (II Kings 3:27) after Mesha in desperation had offered his own son as a human sacrifice.

The Omride dynasty was replaced by Jehu (842–15), another usurper. Jehu found it expedient to submit to the Assyrian king Shalmaneser III. The latter's famed Black Obelisk, now in the British Museum, depicts a bearded figure in a long, fringed tunic bowing down before the Assyrian king. The superscription reads: "The tribute of Jehu, son of Omri. Silver, gold, a golden bowl, a golden vase, golden cups, golden buckets, tin, a staff for the royal hand (?), . . . fruits."[100] The bearded figure may represent the king's representative or the king himself. In the latter case this would be the only pictorial representation of an Israelite king in our possession. Jehu may have been seeking Assyrian help against Hazael, king of Damascus, who was beginning to attack Israel (II Kings 10:32).

Later the son of Hazael, Ben-Hadad, also began to oppress Israel in the days of Joash (801–786), but the Lord gave Israel deliverance (II Kings 13:24–25). An Aramaic stele found in 1907, twenty-five miles south of Aleppo, sheds light on this deliverance. The stele celebrates the victory of Zakir, the ruler of Hamath and Lu'ash south of Aleppo, over Ben-Hadad. Zakir providentially attacked Ben-Hadad from the north at the same time that he was engaged in fighting Israel to the south.[101]

A period of Assyrian weakness allowed Israel to enjoy the long and prosperous reign of Jeroboam II (786–46). But this was cut short by the rise to power of the energetic Assyrian king Tiglath-pileser III (also called Pul). In 739 Menahem of Israel along with Rezin of Damascus and other kings paid tribute to the Assyrians according to the annals of Tiglath-pileser. The corresponding biblical passage (II Kings 15:19 ff.) indicates that Menahem extracted fifty shekels of silver from every able-bodied man—this was the ransom equal to the price of a first-class slave in Assyria at this time. If the total of 1,000 talents—which is equal to 3,600,000 shekels —is divided by fifty shekels, it indicates that Menahem might have been able to muster a force of 70,000 men. Mallowan found at Fort Shalmaneser at Nimrud an arsenal, where a docket listed 36,242 bows. This would indicate that the Assyrian army would have numbered more than 100,000 men.

Unwise as it turned out, Pekah of Israel joined Rezin of Damascus in an anti-Assyrian coalition and tried to forcibly press Jehoahaz (Ahaz) of Judah to join them (II Kings 16:1–6). In order to secure relief Ahaz sent gifts to Tiglath-pileser to save him from his foes. The Assyrian king, who probably needed little excuse, responded. He destroyed Damascus in 732 B.C., and proceeded south, taking Hazor (II Kings 15:29). He boasts in his records: "Pekah their king they deposed and Hosea I set (as king) over them."[102] The Assyrians evidently instigated Pekah's murder (II Kings 15:30 ff.). In the burnt remains of Hazor destroyed by Tiglath-pileser was found a wine jar inscribed "for Pekah."

Shalmaneser V (727–22), the son of Tiglath-pileser III,

continued campaigns against the West. No annals of this king have been recovered, but from a broken text we know that he besieged Samaria for three years because of Hosea's failure to pay tribute. Now the Bible (II Kings 17:3–6) credits the capture of Samaria to "the king of Assyria," who is presumably Shalmaneser V mentioned earlier in the passage. His successor Sargon II, however, claims credit for the capture of Samaria in his annals from Khorsabad. Because of this discrepancy Parrot believed that II Kings was in error.[103] Recent studies have shown that the biblical account is actually the correct version. According to Hallo:

> Shalmaneser V died in December of the same year (722), i.e. *after* the fall of Samaria, and those scholars who, like Olmstead, argued that II Kings 17:6 and 18:10 implied as much seem now definitely to be proven right. Although Sargon may have shared as second-in-command in the siege of Samaria, he misappropriated his predecessor's triumph late in his own reign in order to fill the gap in military activities that, in the earlier records of his reign, loomed in his first year.[104]

In his version Sargon claims to have captured 27,280 persons. "I gave orders," he writes, "that the rest should be settled in the midst of Assyria." He continues: "I restored the city of Samaria and made (it) more habitable than before. I brought into it people from the countries conquered by my own hands."[105] These newcomers formed the mixed population known as the Samaritans. As for the deported ten tribes, they disappeared from history as a separate entity. Unlike the Jews of the southern kingdom whose faith in Jehovah enabled them to retain their identity and to return from exile, the Israelites who had apostasized became completely assimilated with their pagan Assyrian captors.

In 712 Sargon's forces invaded Palestine to suppress a revolt led by Yamani (whose name possibly means "Ionian" Greek), ruler of Ashdod on the Philistine coast. Isa. 20:1

reads: "In the year that Tartan came unto Ashdod, when Sargon the king of Assyria sent him, and fought against Ashdod, and took it." Tartan is not a proper name but is the Assyrian word for a field marshal. As some of the Assyrian records seem to indicate that Sargon led the campaign in person, the biblical account could be understood as mistaken. However, in the case of Assyrian and Egyptian royal inscriptions one always has to take into account the royal vanity which seeks to claim as much as possible for the king. In this case there is other Assyrian evidence that the Bible is correct. Hallo points out that: "Sargon stayed 'in the land' according to the Eponym Chronicle, which confirms Isaiah's statement that his commander-in-chief, the *Turtanu*, led the operations, against the claims of Sargon's annalists . . ., that he personally led the operation."[106] The recent excavations at Ashdod revealed the grim evidence of thirty skeletons crowded in a small room, probably the victims of the Assyrian attack. The prize find at Ashdod was the discovery in 1963 of three fragments of an Assyrian stele commemorating Sargon's victory.

The next Assyrian conqueror to menace Judah was the famous Sennacherib (705–682). It was in preparation for a possible Assyrian attack that Hezekiah built the Siloam Tunnel in Jerusalem (II Kings 20:20; II Chron. 32:30). The tunnel was intended to channel water from the Gihon spring underground into the city. The tunnel is 1,749 feet long and averages about six feet in height. It may still be traversed today if one does not mind wading hip-deep in water. At the end of the nineteenth century a boy swimming in the Pool of Siloam, into which the tunnel debouches, discovered an inscription of Hezekiah which describes the completion of his tunnel:

. . . And this is the story of the piercing through. While (the stone-cutters were swinging their) axes, each towards his fellow, and while there were yet three cubits (4¹/₂ feet) to be pierced through, (there was heard) the voice of a man calling to his fellow . . . .[107]

When the invasion did take place in 701, Sennacherib sent his Tartan, Rab-saris, and Rab-shakeh (these are names of officials and not proper names) to Jerusalem to threaten and frighten the people into surrendering. These officials spoke directly to the people in Hebrew in order to cajole them into surrendering instead of speaking to Hezekiah's officials in Aramaic (II Kings 18:26). A striking parallel to the entire biblical episode is now provided by a letter from the imperial chancery at Nimrud (Calah) addressed to Tiglath-Pileser, who reigned about twenty-five years before Sennacherib. Two generals report on the siege of Babylon to the king as follows:

> On the twenty-eighth we came to Babylon. We stood in front of the Marduk gate. We negotiated with the Babylonian ruler. . . . A servant of Ukin-zer the Chaldean was at his side. They came out with the Babylonian citizens and were standing in front of the gate. We spoke in these terms to the Babylonian citizens: "Why should you act hostilely to us for the sake of them? . . . I am coming to Babylon to confirm your citizen-privileges." We spoke many words with them . . . . They would not agree. They would not come out; they would not talk with us. They kept sending us messages. We said to them: "Open the great gate; let us enter Babylon."[108]

A comparison of the accounts of the Assyrian sieges of Babylon and of Jerusalem prompts Saggs to affirm: "These close and detailed parallels between the two incidents warn against too readily adopting the assumption of captious critics that the speech giving the Rabshakeh's surrender terms 'was a free composition of the (biblical) narrator.'"[109]

Furthermore, the Assyrian practice of using, as at Babylon, an initial token force to demand surrender and of only bringing in the main army in case of non-compliance makes it unnecessary, in Saggs' opinion, to postulate two invasions of Jerusalem as some scholars have proposed. Now we are informed of the campaign of Sennacherib against Jerusalem in 701 from the Bible (II Kings 18–19; Isa. 36–37), and from Sennacherib's records. Because of the differences in these two accounts Albright has suggested that there were two campaigns: the first which the Assyrians won, and the second which ended in disaster for them. This theory is based in part on the reference to the intervention of Tirhakah, king of Ethiopia, i.e. the Cushite or Negroid king of Egypt (II Kings 19:9; Isa. 37:9). Until recently scholars had assumed that Tirhakah would have been too young to have campaigned in 701, and that the reference to his activity must therefore belong to a later campaign. He is known to have become king in 690 B.C. Kitchen now informs us that: "A much improved treatment of the Kawa texts by Leclant and Yoyotte, published in 1952, alters this completely and would allow Tirhakah to be about twenty or twenty-one-years-old in 701 B.C., which makes him quite old enough to act on behalf of his brother, King Shebitku . . . ."[110]

We may therefore consider that there was but one campaign which was reported differently by the two sides. Both sources place Hezekiah's tribute at thirty talents of gold. But only 300 talents of silver are recorded in the biblical account compared with 800 in the Assyrian text. The divergence may be due to a textual corruption, or to differences between the measures used, or different items reckoned. The Assyrian account in the Taylor Prism now in the British Museum reads:

But as for *Ha-za-qi-ia-u* (Hezekiah), the Jew, who did not bow in submission to my yoke, forty-six of his strong walled towns and innumerable smaller villages in their neighborhood I besieged and conquered (cf. II Kings 18:13) by stamping down earth-ramps and then by bringing up battering rams, by the assault of foot-soldiers, by breaches, tunnelling and sapper operations. . . . He himself I shut up like a caged bird within Jerusalem his royal city.[111]

Sennacherib, however, did not have the satisfaction of taking Jerusalem. According to the biblical account, celebrated in Lord Byron's well-known poem, the angel of the Lord suddenly smote the Assyrian horde. A reflection of this catastrophe may be contained in the garbled account of Herodotus (II:141) that the Assyrian army at the borders of

9. The Cyrus Cylinder, which announces the liberation by Cyrus of the city of Babylon (*Courtesy, The British Museum.*)

Egypt was attacked by a multitude of field mice. Some scholars have seen in this the suggestion of bubonic plague, which is known to have afflicted the ancient world on several occasions.

Though Sennacherib was not able to take Jerusalem he did capture the great fortress at Lachish—a feat which he proudly recorded in reliefs at Nineveh. The excavations at Lachish have produced some interesting evidence. In the debris in the lower roadway was found the crest of a bronze helmet with traces of cloth and leather, identical to those worn in the reliefs by the Assyrian soldiers. Fragments of Assyrian armor and arrows were also found.[112] Barnett has recently made an interesting observation concerning the fate of some of the Lachish captives. Examining some of the reliefs from Sennacherib's palace at Nineveh, he finds that men with the peculiar headdresses of the Lachish Jews are found serving in the bodyguard of the Assyrian king. Barnett further speculates that in the palace revolt which took place at Sennacherib's death, the person who defaced the king's face in the reliefs may have been a Lachishite Jew who had served the king out of expediency but who now showed his spite by this action.[113]

After his deliverance from the Assyrians, Hezekiah fell ill. During this illness he received messengers and a present from Merodach-Baladan, king of Babylon (II Kings 20:12–18; Isa. 39:1–8; II Chron. 32:31). The Chaldean king was acting not out of solicitude for the Jewish king's health, but was in reality seeking allies against his Assyrian overlords. Both Sargon II and Sennacherib tried repeatedly to suppress this wily foe. Cuneiform records indicate that Merodach-Baladan was more of a clever politician than a courageous warrior; he bribed the Elamites of southwestern Persia to do most of his fighting for him.[114]

Late in the seventh century the Neo-Babylonians with the

aid of the Persians were able to overthrow the Assyrians. Nineveh fell in 612, and an Assyrian remnant tried to hold out in Haran until 610. It was in a futile attempt to block Egyptian aid to the embattled Assyrians that Josiah, king of Judah, met his death at Megiddo in 609 (II Kings 23:29). The verse should be translated accordingly: "Pharaoh Necho king of Egypt went up to (rather than against) the king of Assyria . . . ."

In 605 the great Nebuchadnezzar succeeded his father as king of Babylon. A few months before his accession Nebuchadnezzar defeated the Egyptian king Necho at Carchemish in northwestern Mesopotamia. Excavations here by Woolley and Lawrence ("of Arabia") turned up evidence of this battle, including an Ionian shield which belonged to a Greek mercenary fighting for the Egyptians. Greek mercenaries, including the brother of the famous poet Alcaeus, were also fighting for the Babylonians.[115]

In 1942 an Aramaic papyrus was found in a jar at Saqqara in Egypt. It was a letter from a king called Adon to a pharaoh. Adon, who is probably the king of Askalon, seems to be asking for aid from Necho against the invading forces of Nebuchadnezzar (II Kings 23–24). The letter which is dated *c.* 604 is with the exception of a mutilated fragment the oldest Aramaic papyrus known, and as such is important for its bearing on the Aramaic portions of the Old Testament. John Bright suggests why:

The Aramaic of Ezra (4:8–6:18, 7:12–26), which contains correspondence purportedly with the Persian court and in Aramaic, and which has been branded as a forgery by such able scholars as C. C. Torrey (*Ezra Studies* [1910], pp. 140 ff.) and R. H. Pfeiffer (*Introduction to the Old Testament* [1941], pp. 816 ff.), takes on a more authentic flavor with each such discovery. Again, that courtiers should address Nebuchadnezzar in Aramaic as the story in Dan. 2:4 has it, no longer appears at all surprising.[116]

One of the last of the kings of Judah, Jehoiakim (609–598), seems to have owed his position to the Egyptians. Against the advice of Jeremiah he fomented revolt against the Babylonians. The prophet also rebuked the king for oppressing the people, and for building a luxurious palace with the fruits of his oppression (Jer. 22:13 ff.). Just south of Jerusalem at Ramat Rahel, Aharoni has found remains of a palace which fit the description of Jehoiakim's building. The excavator suggests that the king built this stronghold to protect himself against the populace who resented his reign.[117]

Important texts of the late seventh and early sixth century, called the Babylonian or the Chaldean Chronicles, were published by D. J. Wiseman in 1956. In contrast to the usually biased royal documents, these Chronicles are remarkably objective. The new texts provide an explanation for Dan. 1:1, which speaks of an otherwise unattested attack on Jerusalem in Nebuchadnezzar's first year, Jehoiakim's third year. (The chronology is complicated by the use of two regnal dating systems.) The Chronicle reveals that after Nebuchadnezzar defeated Necho at Carchemish he proceeded south: "In the accession-year Nebuchadnezzar went back again to the Hatti-land (Syria and Palestine) and marched victoriously through it until the month of Sebat (spring, 604). In the month of Sebat he took the heavy tribute of the Hattiland back to Babylon."[118] Daniel and Ezekiel were evidently among those in this first deportation.

The Chronicles also reveal a hitherto unknown battle of 601 in which the Egyptians defeated the Babylonians. This may explain why Jehoiakim ceased to pay tribute to Babylon (II Kings 24:1) and disregarding the advice of Jeremiah (37:6 ff.) turned for help to the "bruised reed" of Egypt. Thanks to the Babylonian Chronicle we can precisely date the ensuing capture of Jerusalem by the Babylonians to March 16, 597, three months after the death of Jehoiakim. The biblical account (II Chron. 36:10) corresponds exactly with the Babylonian text. After Nebuchadnezzar had taken the city and captured Jehoiachin, the new king, the Babylonian source informs us that: "He appointed therein a king of his own choice, received its heavy tribute and sent (them) to Babylon."[119] The puppet king was Jehoiachin's uncle Mattaniah, whose name was changed to Zedekiah (II Kings 24:17).

The third attack of the Babylonians in 587 involved the destruction of Jerusalem and its temple. The tense situation of this period is depicted in the Lachish Ostraca, letters written on broken pieces of pottery. One of these letters carries the dramatic message, "And (my lord) will know that we are watching for the signals of Lachish, according to all the signs which my lord hath given, for we cannot see Azekah."[120] This may mean that the fortress of Azekah, which was halfway between Lachish and Jerusalem, had already fallen to the Babylonians (Jer. 34:7).

The devastation wrought by the Babylonians may be seen from the archaeological evidence. Kenyon notes that:

Large numbers of towns were destroyed and never occupied again. . . . There had been periods of intermission of occupation of sites previously, but at no other time had large numbers of sites ceased permanently to be towns. This shows clearly how disastrous an effect the Babylonian policy had on the economy of the country.[121]

H. The Exile and The Post-Exilic Period

It is difficult for us now to believe that late in the nineteenth century and early in our century there was a serious attempt by some scholars, notably by C. C. Torrey of Yale, to discredit the biblical accounts of the Babylonian attack on Judah and the subsequent Exile. The entire history of the sixth–fifth centuries B.C. was rewritten by critics who rejected as unhistorical the writings of Chronicles, Ezra, Ezekiel, and even Jeremiah. Albright, who already in the 1920's opposed this trend, writes:

> Of all aberrations of historical criticism, the attempt—beginning in the 1890's—to discredit the traditional picture of the total destruction of Judah by the Babylonians and their allies between 597 and 582 B.C. is one of the most extraordinary. This necessarily involved rejection of the historicity of the Restoration. There would thus be no Captivity and no Return from Exile in any conventional sense. In order to reach such radical conclusions, Chronicles was dated to the third century B.C. and its stylistic affinity to the Ezra memoirs in the first person was thought to prove that the latter were spurious.[122]

Excavations have once again vindicated the biblical record against hypothetical reconstructions. Virtually all of the fortified towns in Judah were destroyed, including Jerusalem, Tell Beit Mirsim, Lachish, Beth-shemesh, Ramat Rahel, Bethel, Tell enNasbeh. Of all the excavated cities only Samaria and Gezer have revealed fairly continuous occupation throughout the Exilic and post-Exilic periods. Of a population of 250–300,000 in eighth century Judah, only about half probably survived the onslaught. Moreover the borders of the state of Judah were severely contracted. Saul Weinberg in a recent survey of the evidence comments: "So elementary must this existence have been that it has proved extremely difficult to pick up its traces in material remains."[123]

Among the arguments used by Torrey in his *Pseudo-Ezekiel and the Original Prophecy* (1930) against the biblical picture of the Exile was the dating of Ezekiel's prophecies by the years of Jehoiachin's captivity. He also argued that the prophet could not have referred to the Persians before they had appeared on the historical scene. The first doubtful point was confirmed by the discovery of several seals bearing the inscription "Belonging to Eliakim, steward of Yaukin (for Jehoiachin)," found at Tell Beit Mirsim and at Beth-shemesh. This indicates that despite the fact that he had reigned but three short months in Judah the Jews continued to regard Jehoiachin even in exile as their legitimate monarch. Then in 1932 Ernst Weidner published tablets from Babylon which list the distribution of rations in oil, sesame, and barley to various captives—including Yaukin, king of Judah (cf. II Kings 25:27–30). This is an explicit confirmation of the biblical record. As to Torrey's other point, he was not aware that Assyrian tablets had already been published referring to the Persians a century before Ezekiel's time.[124]

After the capture of Babylon in 539 by the Persians, the Bible reports that Cyrus the Great magnanimously permitted the Jews who wanted to return to Palestine to do so, and even aided them with supplies. Oesterly and Robinson in their history of Israel published in 1932 regarded this account with suspicion. There is every reason now to believe from all that we know of Cyrus that this gracious dispensation to the Jews was entirely in accord with his general policy toward various religions. Even to the vanquished city of Babylon and its god he displayed the utmost deference, as he tells us in the so-called "Cyrus Cylinder":

> When I, well-disposed, entered Babylon, I set up the seat of dominion in the royal palace amidst jubilation and rejoicing. Marduk the great god caused the big-hearted inhabitants of Babylon to . . . me. I sought daily to worship him. My numerous troops moved about undisturbed in the midst of Babylon. I did not allow any to terrorize the land of [Sumer] and Akkad. I kept in view the needs of Babylon and all its sanctuaries to promote their well-being.[125]

In a text discovered at Ur, Cyrus also shows reverence toward that city's moon god Sin. At Uruk inscriptions show that the temple of Ishtar was rebuilt by Cyrus.

The decree of Cyrus is recorded in Ezra 1:2–4 in Hebrew and in Ezra 6:3–5 in Aramaic. Although some historians were skeptical, Eduard Meyer in 1869 had already accepted this account as genuine. The discovery of the Aramaic papyri from Elephantine, in upper Egypt, a generation later, vindicated his claim. Freedman, assessing the value of the Elephantine Papyri, comments: "They offer a solid basis of comparison with the Aramaic portions of Ezra. So far as language is concerned, there is no reason to doubt the authenticity of the reports in the biblical book."[126] There is reason to believe that the Hebrew version was intended for distribution to the Jews, whereas the Aramaic version may have been an official memorandum for storage in the archives of Ecbatana (Ezra 6:2).[127]

When Nehemiah, the Persian king's cupbearer, came to inspect the ruins of Jerusalem in the middle of the fifth century, he found that his donkey's path was blocked by rubble. Kenyon's recent excavations have vividly illustrated this situation, and have also shown that the rapid repair of the walls in fifty-two days was made possible by the drastic contraction of the city's circuit in Nehemiah's day.

Among those who opposed Nehemiah's work was Geshem or Gashmu the Arabian (Neh. 2:19; 6:1,2,6). The Brooklyn Museum has acquired eight silver vessels, three with Aramaic inscriptions, from the Delta region of Egypt. One of the inscriptions reads: "That which Qainu bar Geshem, king of Qedar, brought in offering to han-'Ilat."[128] Qedar (Jer. 49:28) was in northwest Arabia. Since Cambyses had employed the Arabians in his conquest of Egypt in 525 the Arab chieftains had maintained good relations with the Persians. This is why Geshem's opposition to Nehemiah was important.

C. C. Torrey's belief that the words for coins in Ezra 2:69, 8:27, and Nehemiah 7:70–72 were references to Greek drachmas led him to date the works of the so-called Chronicler—Ezra, Nehemiah, and Chronicles—to about 250 B.C.[129] Weingreen, on the other hand, holds that these passages refer to the Persian *daric*, a gold coin minted by Darius the Great (522–487 B.C.), and argues that these references are indeed "proof that the accounts given in these memoirs were written at a time close to the events which they describe."[130] Whether these terms refer to the Persian *daric* or to the Greek *drachma*, their occurence in Ezra and Nehemiah do not make these references anachronistic as Greek coins appear in Palestine already in the Persian period. Excavations at Beth-zur in 1931 and subsequent finds have turned up Greek drachmas or atticizing imitations from the fifth century.

One Old Testament book whose alleged late date most critics have not reconsidered is the book of Daniel. Its composition is commonly dated to 165 B.C. on the assumption that it is a pseudonymous work written to encourage the Maccabean Jews in their struggle against the Seleucids. A number of arguments have been used to support this contention: 1) It is alleged that "Darius the Mede" is not identifiable with any historic person and that he represents a confusion with Darius the Persian. 2) The book does not name Nabonidus as the last king of Babylon but his son Belshazzar instead. 3) The madness of Nebuchadnezzar is thought to be a transference of the erratic behavior of Nabonidus. 4) Its literary form resembles the later apocalyptic works. 5) Greek loan words seem to indicate a late date. 6) Its description of the historical situation which prevailed in the second century with Antiochus IV is too accurate to be prophecy; it must therefore be *vaticinium ex eventu* or prophecy after the event.

Rowley has argued that the writer of Daniel has erroneously thought of a Median empire earlier than the Persian one, and mistakenly called Darius (the Persian) a Mede.[131] Whitcomb, following a suggestion of Albright, has tried to identify the biblical "Darius the Mede" with the Gubaru of the cuneiform sources who was a provincial governor.[132] Most recently, D. J. Wiseman on the basis of new inscriptions from Harran has proposed that "Darius the Mede" could have been a title for Cyrus the Persian. Cyrus was himself half Median and half Persian. In 550 he overthrew his Median grandfather, but still retained Medes in his court. In the new Harran inscriptions Nabonidus in 546 speaks of the "King of the Medes" who must be Cyrus.[133]

For a long time the fact that Daniel mentioned as the last king of Babylon not Nabonidus but Belshazzar puzzled scholars. For some time even Belshazzar's identity was questioned until it was shown that he was Nabonidus' son. It was not until 1924 when Sidney Smith published the "Persian Verse Account" that scholars took seriously the intimation that Nabonidus had spent several years in the Arabian desert.

In 1956 D. S. Rice discovered three stelae at Haran which had been used as thresholds by the Muslims in their mosque. These important inscriptions describe the death of the mother of Nabonidus, a remarkable woman who lived to be 104. Nabonidus came originally from Haran and was fanatically dedicated to its moon god Sin, to the point where he neglected the service of Marduk the patron god of Babylon. After rebuilding the temple of Sin at Haran the king inexplicably removed himself to the oasis of Tema in northwestern Arabia, leaving Babylon in the hands of Belshazzar.

Nabonidus, however, had not abdicated. He is still called *sharru* or "king," and gives orders from Tema to Belshazzar. Before leaving for Tema, Nabonidus had "entrusted kingship (*sharrutam*)" to his son. It is petty to object as Rowley does that Belshazzar was not *de jure* king; as far as the Jews in Babylon were concerned he was certainly *de facto* king. The elevation of Daniel as the "third ruler" (Dan. 5:29) seems to be a recognition of the situation with two rulers above him. Dougherty, who made a comprehensive study of the cuneiform texts dealing with Nabonidus and Belshazzar, concludes that "of all non-Babylonian records dealing with the situation at the close of the Neo-Babylonian Empire, the fifth chapter of Daniel ranks next to cuneiform literature in accuracy so far as outstanding events are concerned."[134]

Some scholars have proposed the thesis that the story of Nebuchadnezzar's madness in Daniel is a distorted reflection of Nabonidus' exile in Arabia. It is now clear from the new Harran inscriptions that Nabonidus was in exile for ten years and not for seven as had been thought previously (Dan. 4:32 speaks of "seven times"). Among other objections to this interpretation is the point that this theory was based on Sidney Smith's rendering of a line in the Persian Verse Account: "an evil demon (*shedu*) had altered him." According to this rendering, Nabonidus went to Arabia because he was mad. The latest translation by Oppenheim now renders this line: "(his) protective deity became hostile to him."[135]

Now Nabonidus' behavior may seem erratic to us but that is because of our modern prejudices. The new Harran texts finally give us the reason for his self-exile to Tema. We learn that: "the sons of Babylon, . . . priests (and) people of the capitals of Akkad, against his great divinity (Sin) offended . . . treason and not loyalty, like a dog they devoured one another; fever and famine in the midst of them . . . ."[136] Nabonidus refused to return to Babylon, a city which he considered cursed by Sin for the disrespect shown to that deity, until the Babylonians should show some signs of repentance.

Although it may resemble late apocalyptic writings Daniel is not necessarily derived from them. It is more probable that they were patterned after Daniel. Akkadian prototypes of Daniel's prophecies are known from the early second millennium. Grayson and Lambert write: "It is interesting to note that the book of Daniel has many similarities to the *Akkadian Prophecies.*"[137] As far as the narration of Daniel's rise-fall-and-rise as the wise counselor is concerned, this has its parallel in an undisputed fifth century Aramaic document, the story of Ahiqar. It is now quite certain that Ahiqar was a historic figure at the Assyrian court of the seventh century.

The argument from the presence of Greek loan words in Daniel is the most objective basis for a late date. This was formulated by S. R. Driver in 1897, who claimed that the Greek words demanded a date after the conquest of Palestine by Alexander the Great, late in the fourth century B.C. Since the time of Driver's statement there has been a flood of materials to show that contacts between the Aegean and the Near East began long before the time of Alexander.

The Greeks of Cilicia and Cyprus came into direct contact with Mesopotamia as the result of Assyrian expansion to the northwest in the eighth and seventh centuries. The Greek rulers of these areas sent contributions to Assyria; other Greeks were used in the Assyrian navy. In the seventh century, Greek mercenaries were used by Egypt to rid itself of the Assyrians. We have already seen that Greek mercenaries were used both by Necho and by Nebuchadnezzar at the end of the seventh century. New evidence has now come to light to indicate that Greek mercenaries were also being used in Palestine at this time.

In 1960 the site of Mesad Hashavyahu between Ashdod and Jaffa was excavated. This proved to be a small fort established by Greeks about 630–25 as evidenced by the large quantity of Greek pottery. The settlers were probably Greek mercenaries employed by Psammetichus I of Egypt. The fort was conquered by Josiah a few years before 609.[138] Far inland just west of the Dead Sea at Arad, ostraca have been discovered from the stratum which was destroyed by

Nebuchadnezzar in 598. These ostraca mention supplies given to the *Kittim*, whom Aharoni considers to be Greek mercenaries serving in the remote forts of Judah.[139]

Nebuchadnezzar also employed Greek craftsmen.[140] The walls of the king's throne room at Babylon were decorated with Ionic (Greek) capitals. Greeks, probably Cypriotes, were well known to Nabonidus. At Babylon one Greek sherd of the seventh century and sherds of nine Greek vessels of the sixth century have been found. Elements of Greek style may be seen in the architecture of Pasargadai, the palace which Cyrus built *c.* 550. Cyrus, who conquered Lydia and Ionia in 546, used numerous Ionian Greeks in his building activities, as did his successors Darius and Xerxes.[141] In the light of the widespread Greek contacts before Alexander, we would conclude that the Greek words in Daniel can no longer be used as evidence for a late date.[142]

The single argument which remains for a late date for Daniel is the striking correspondence with the events of the Maccabean period. If one rejects beforehand the possibility of prophecy, this is an irrefutable argument. Now it is certain that there were cases in Egypt and Mesopotamia of prophecies after the event for the purpose of political propaganda. But whether any given ancient prophecy was made after the event must be proved by other criteria, and not initially assumed. We believe that other criteria indicate that the book of Daniel was the work of a true prophet, and not the product of a Maccabean ghost writer.[143]

II

RAMSEY VS. THE TÜBINGEN SCHOOL: *The Confirmation of the New Testament*

Is the New Testament a collection of theological writings with little relationship to history? How authentic are the so-called "Holy Sites" in Palestine? Where was Jesus crucified and buried? Can we actually walk in "the steps of Paul"? Have Peter's bones been found?

A. The Tübingen School and Form Criticism

In New Testament criticism the scholar who corresponds in stature and influence to Julius Wellhausen in Old Testament studies is F. C. Baur of Tübingen (1792–1860). Like Wellhausen, Baur seems to have been influenced by Hegel's philosophy.[1] The philosophic dialectic of Hegel assumed that history went through a pattern of thesis—antithesis—synthesis. According to Baur, Paul representing Gentile Christianity (thesis) advocated freedom from the law. Peter's party representing Jewish Christianity (antithesis) and advocating adherance to the law was the group that reacted against Paul's teaching. From this conflict emerged a synthesis of the second century church (as seen in Acts).

Like Wellhausen in the field of Old Testament criticism,

Baur having established an evolutionary scheme of development believed that he could date the New Testament documents according to their place in this pattern. On this basis he accepted only four of the epistles as genuinely Pauline (Galatians, Romans, I and II Corinthians). John's Gospel was placed as late as the second half of the second century. The Acts of the Apostles was also assigned this late date. Its author was not writing history but was trying to produce a certain effect by his imaginative description of the early Church. Baur's views were quite dominant throughout the nineteenth century and have left a lasting legacy for the twentieth century, though many of his assumptions have been disproved.

Johannes Munck of Denmark has underscored the baneful effects of this legacy. He argues that the Tübingen concept of a struggle between Jewish-Christian nomism and Gentile-Christian antinomism has now been compressed by scholars into the thirty years between the death of Jesus and the death of Paul. How this pervasive influence affects New Testament scholarship is illustrated by Munck:

> In dividing up primitive Christianity into Jewish Christianity on the one hand and Paul and Gentile Christianity on the other hand, it has been made nearly impossible to understand the early church in Palestine and Paul. . . . Thus the different parts of the New Testament are like completely watertight compartments thanks to a school which no one believes to be of interest for our modern research . . . .[2]

Munck cites Gal. 2:1–10 which informs us of a concordat between Paul and Peter, and asserts that the conflict ascribed to these two is but a scholar's myth. He further complains that this myth has become almost a dogma with liberal New Testament scholars.[3]

The Tübingen School was followed by the *Religions-*

geschichtliche or "History of Religions" School, which in Pauline research emphasized parallels with pagan mystery religions. These scholars concluded that Christianity was the product of various syncretistic influences. Jesus was interpreted in terms of Jewish apocalypticism. W. Bousset held that the church in Palestine, which was thoroughly Jewish, considered Jesus as simply an exalted man. It was only with the spread of Christianity to the Gentile world that Jesus was worshiped as divine. Paul's Greek orientation was opposed to the Jewish Jesus, and Paul's own concepts of Christ were supposedly borrowed from the Hellenistic mysteries.

Form criticism, which is the consideration of the various literary units, was applied to the New Testament as well as to the Old Testament with similar negative results. The dominant figure in recent studies has been Rudolf Bultmann, who used the form critical method with the presuppositions of the History of Religions School. For Bultmann the bulk of the Gospel materials are the late creations of the church, aetiological legends as it were. He distinguishes between the *historische Jesus* (the human Jesus who walked the roads of Palestine) and the *geschichtliche Christus* (the Christ of faith who gives meaning to history). The former is virtually unknowable; it is the latter that can be apprehended by faith. The Gospel of John, which is explained by Mandaean parallels, is late and completely unhistorical.[4] In the words of Vincent Taylor, extreme form critics like Bultmann practically assume that all eyewitnesses were taken out of the world at the time of the ascension of the Lord.

According to form critics like Bultmann and Dibelius, the various miracle stories, parables, passion accounts, etc. were passed on orally for many years. The so-called *Redaktionsgeschichte* or "Redactional History" scholars attempt to analyze how the various authors or editors have put these literary units together to support their theological views. It is commonly assumed that the Evangelists and the writer of Acts were interested in theology and not in history.[5]

As in the case of Old Testament literary criticism, New Testament literary criticism was born in pre-archaeological days. The Tübingen School flourished during a time when hardly anything was known about the chronology of Greek pottery or Hellenistic—Roman architecture. A disregard for archaeological data characterizes even the later form critical school. As Albright notes:

> In the same way, the form-critical school founded by M. Dibelius and R. Bultmann a generation before the discovery of the Dead Sea Scrolls has continued to flourish without the slightest regard for the Dead Sea Scrolls. In other words, all radical schools in New Testament criticism which have existed in the past or which exist today are pre-archaeological, and are, therefore, since they were built *in der Luft* ("in the air"), quite antiquated today.[6]

The first to see that the archaeological facts did not fit the theories of scholars but rather confirmed the New Testament itself was the great archaeologist of Asia Minor, William Ramsay. When he began his researches in Asia Minor at the end of the nineteenth century he had accepted the views of the then dominant Tübingen School, as he informs us:

> On the contrary, I began with a mind unfavorable to it (Acts), for the ingenuity and apparent completeness of the Tübingen theory had at one time quite convinced me. It did not lie then in my line of life to investigate the subject minutely; but more recently I found myself often brought into contact with the book of Acts as an authority for the topography, antiquities, and society of Asia Minor. It was gradually borne in upon me that in various details the narrative showed marvelous truth. In fact, beginning with the fixed idea that the work was essentially a second century composition, and never relying on its evidence as trustworthy for first century conditions, I gradually came to find it a useful ally in some obscure and difficult investigations.[7]

The Stones and The Scriptures

Despite the undoubted stature of Ramsay as the leading authority on Roman Asia Minor, the ingrained prejudices of liberal New Testament scholars did not permit them to readily accept his views in support of the New Testament. Olmstead, a leading ancient historian of recent days, comments on this situation:

> These books (of Ramsay) had a great vogue in his own day and are still re-read by professional students of the ancient world. To them, it seems unbelievable that they met an almost universally hostile reception from contemporary critics. In their eyes, they alone were competent to expound the New Testament; how dared a confessed outsider to invade with profane foot the sacred precinct, . . . and even assert that *professional* New Testament scholars were wrong in method and in results?[8]

When, thanks to Ramsay's works, other scholars came to a more positive appreciation of the work of Luke as a historian, their views were in turn rejected by critical New Testament scholars. As Gasque points out:

> Zahn was, of course, a conservative and therefore regarded as "uncritical". Harnack's increasingly conservative conclusions regarding Acts were written off as merely one of his eccentric opinions. . . . Eduard Meyer had the unfortunate disadvantage of coming to the study of Acts "with the presuppositions of a historian of antiquity," thus misunderstanding, "the nature of its accounts and the way in which they are connected".[9]

A. T. Ehrhardt, who served as lecturer in Roman and Civil Law at Freiburg University before becoming a lecturer in church history at Manchester University writes:

> In the field of the literary criticism of the Book of Acts it seems almost incomprehensible how lightly theologians have dismissed the thesis of Eduard Meyer, who maintained that St. Luke figures as the one great historian who joins the last of the genuinely Greek historians, Polybius, to the first great Christian historian, perhaps

the greatest of all, Eusebius of Caesarea. The man who proposed this view was after all the last European scholar who possessed the learning to write an Ancient History of his own. It seems too easy to dismiss his views with invective about "Historisimus" . . . .[10]

We have today the ironic situation in which some New Testament scholars who have been guided by axioms of literary criticism reject the historicity of the New Testament, whereas professional historians of antiquity examining the documents against the background of classical texts and archaeological materials find the New Testament to be historically accurate. G. A. Williamson, the translator of Josephus' *The Jewish War* for the Penguin Classics series, contrasts the speeches of Acts with those found in Josephus as follows:

> Very different are the addresses and conversations recorded in the Acts of the Apostles, in which the author shows a complete familiarity with the thought, expression, and habitual terminology of the speakers, and because he writes at so short an interval of time is able to draw on the memories of speakers or auditors—and what memories the people of that time possessed!—if not on written notes, which we have reason to believe were commonly made.[11]

B. H. Warmington, Reader in Ancient History at the University of Bristol, commenting upon the historical sources for Nero's reign, writes: "Lastly may be mentioned Acts and some of the Pauline Epistles in the New Testament. Their importance in describing the early progress of an ultimately dominant religion are obvious. When they deal with aspects of Roman law and government they have long been regarded by historians as reliable."[12] In a similar vein the distinguished Roman historian A. N. Sherwin-White has recently remarked:

> For Acts the confirmation of historicity is overwhelming. . . . Any attempt to reject its basic historicity even in matters of detail

must now appear absurd. Roman historians have long taken it for granted.[13]

B. Jesus of Nazareth

One of the most controversial questions as to the accuracy of Luke concerns the Christmas census. It is now certain that Jesus was born before 4 B.C., the date of the death of Herod the Great, as it was to Herod that the magi came in search for the newborn king. It is the familiar words of Luke 2:2 that poses a problem: "And this taxing (enrollment) was first made when Cyrenius (Quirinius) was governor of Syria."

Now a census under Quirinius as governor of Syria is well-known for A.D. 6 but none is known for the period before 4 B.C. We do have considerable evidence for periodic censuses of citizens and of non-citizens during the reign of Augustus.[14] In Egypt a census seems to have been taken every fourteen years. The requirement that the person to be enrolled travel to his town of origin has been illustrated by an edict from Egypt. Adolf Deissmann says:

> Perhaps the most remarkable discovery of this kind in the new texts is a singular parallel to the statement in Luke 2:3, which has been so much questioned on the strength of mere book-learning . . . . That this was no mere figment of St. Luke or his authority, but that similar things took place in that age, is proved by an edict of G. Vibius Maximus.[15]

Since such a census as Luke describes could have taken place, the major difficulty that remains is the specific association of Quirinius with an early, unrecorded census. An inscription discovered in Rome in 1828 describes the career of a man who has been identified as Quirinius by Mommsen. The text reads that this individual was a legate (governor) *(I)TERUM SYRIAM*.[16] This was interpreted by Ramsay to mean that Quirinius governed "again Syria," in other words over Syria twice. It can, however, be argued that this only means that Quirinius was legate twice, and that his first position was in Galatia. The difficulty of placing Quirinius as legate in Syria before 4 B.C. is that from other texts we have a fairly complete list of legates. Ramsay therefore suggested that Quirinius may have been attached to the legate Saturninus as an extaordinary legate for military purposes.

In the light of these facts the following solutions have been proposed: 1) F. M. Heichelheim suggested translating Luke 2:2 to read: "This census was the first *before* that under the prefectureship of Quirinius in Syria." This is a very unlikely rendering of the Greek text. 2) As Tertullian asserts that Jesus was born after an enrollment under Saturninus who governed from 9 to 6 B.C., it has been suggested by F. F. Bruce that an early copyist may have mistakenly substituted Quirinius for Saturninus. 3) Jack Finegan accepts Ramsay's proposal and concludes: "In view of the sequence of known events in his (Quirinius) career a likely time might have been in 6 or 5 B.C. That Quirinius actually took this census is still only concretely affirmed by Luke 2:2; under the circumstances, as we have reconstructed them, the affirmation is not unlikely."[17]

Another chronological notice of Luke's which had been thought faulty but which is now known to be correct is his reference in Luke 3:1 to "Lysanias the tetrarch of Abilene" at a time when John the Baptist began his ministry in A.D. 27. As the only ruler of that name who was known from ancient historians was a King Lysanias executed in 36 B.C. Luke seemed to be clearly in error. Two Greek inscriptions from Abila, eighteen miles west, northwest of Damascus, have now proven that there was a "Lysanias the tetrarch" between the years A.D. 14–29.

When we come to examine the places associated with Jesus, we find that in many cases we are dependent upon late traditions and cannot be sure of the authenticity of some of the holy sites. In A.D. 70 Jerusalem was destroyed by Titus, and in A.D. 135 by Hadrian, who made Jerusalem the pagan Aelia Capitolina, which was forbidden territory for any Jews or Christians of Jewish origin. A Gentile Christian community did live on in Jerusalem, however. Our earliest Christian source is the report of Melito, bishop of Sardis (second century). The great scholar Origen (185–254) made a careful investigation of the sites, and this information was systematized by Eusebius of Caesarea (265–340), the famous church historian. From the Pilgrim of Bordeaux (333) and subsequent travelers we have reports that vary in value.

The tradition that Jesus was born at Bethlehem in a cave goes back to Justin Martyr, who was born c. 100 in Neapolis in the area of Samaria. Jerome, the translator of the Vulgate, made his home in 385 in a cave adjacent to the traditional cave of Jesus' birth. He tells us that Hadrian had desecrated the cave by consecrating it with a grove of Tammuz or Adonis, and that Constantine's mother Helena built a church over the spot in the fourth century. Investigations in 1934 and 1948–51 have revealed floor mosaics two and a half feet below the present floor. These may belong to the Constantinian basilica.

Nazareth where Jesus spent his childhood is not mentioned in the Old Testament or in Josephus. Its name was found for the first time on an epigraphical document in excavations at Caesarea. Of the numerous holy sites here none seems to be of certain association, except Mary's well which is fed by the only good spring in Nazareth.

Cana, the site of the first miracle, is pointed out to tourists at Kafr Kenna six miles east of Nazareth on the road to Tiberias. Before the seventeenth century the site of Cana had been located at Khirbet Qana eight miles north of Nazareth. Although the site has not been excavated there are pieces of

10. The pool of Siloam, which is still provided with water from the Gihon Spring through the tunnel of Hezekiah.

pottery from the Roman period on the surface. This is the probable spot of the New Testament Cana, although it is unfortunately not placed in as convenient a location for tourists as Kafr Kenna.

Of certain identification as Capernaum is the site of Tell Hum on the northwest shore of the Sea of Galilee. The famous synagogue was excavated in 1866 by Charles Wilson, and by H. Kohl and C. Watzinger in 1905, who dated the building to A.D. 200. The Franciscan Father, G. Orfali, who conducted work here in 1921, argued that it was the synagogue of the first century (Luke 7:5), but he has not convinced other scholars. The main synagogue building, originally two stories high, is over seventy feet long and fifty feet wide. The second-floor gallery would have been reserved for the women. In the southeast corner below the limestone steps are black basalt blocks which may belong to the synagogue of Jesus' day.

Orfali also excavated a basalt-paved street and found many hand grist mills and olive presses. In 1968 V. Corbo excavated beneath an octagonal basilica of the fifth century, and found the remains of a fishermen's quarter from the first century A.D. On the basis of the graffiti of pilgrims, Corbo believes that he has uncovered the very house of Peter.[18]

North of Capernaum is Kerazeh, biblical Chorazin, also investigated by Kohl and Watzinger. There is a basalt synagogue here of the second-third century A.D. with a "seat of Moses" (Matt. 23:2) for the chief official of the synagogue. With the exception of fragments and the recently discovered synagogue at Masada, all of the synagogue buildings in Palestine date from the second century A.D. and later. Most of the earlier synagogues were destroyed in the two wars against the Romans.

Halfway between Galilee and Judea in Samaria is one site which all authorities believe to be authentic. This is Jacob's

Well where Jesus spoke with the woman of Samaria (John 4). Above it loom the twin mountains of Ebal and of Gerizim. It was the latter which the woman pointed out as the sacred place of worship for the Samaritans.[19] As John's narrative described it, the well is quite deep—about one hundred feet in depth. The well is today enclosed beneath an unfinished Greek Orthodox church.

In Jerusalem there are two pools of water which can with confidence be associated with Jesus' ministry. The first is the Pool of Siloam (John 9:7–11) to which Jesus sent a blind man. The pool is located at the end of Hezekiah's tunnel. The other pool is that of Bethesda, a pool with five porches or

11. The synagogue at Capernaum.

porticoes, at the side of which the lame man lay whom Jesus made whole (John 5:1-14). Early pilgrims had referred to the twin pools of Bethesda but over the centuries their location was lost. Then in 1888 as the White Fathers cleared some ruins on the grounds of the Church of St. Anne, they found an old fresco representing the story of John 5. Below this a flight of steps led down to the pools of Bethesda. Originally this had five porticoes, four on each side and a fifth separating the twin pools. It has been estimated that in Jesus' day the pools were as large as a football field, and about twenty feet deep.

Although it was possible to go directly from Galilee to Jerusalem through Samaria, Jews often took the long way around because of the hostility between the Jews and the Samaritans. Pilgrims would cross into Peraea east of the Jordan and then come up to Jerusalem from Jericho. Kelso's excavations have revealed something of the luxury and splendor of New Testament Jericho. Among other structures uncovered was a great sunken garden 360 feet in length, adorned with statuary niches, reflecting pool, and flower pots which were still in place. The excavator remarks that:

> Everything about this civic center instantly calls up Rome and Pompeii. Indeed, one might say that here in New Testament Jericho is a section of Augustan Rome that has been miraculously transferred on a magic carpet from the banks of the Tiber to the banks of the Wadi Qelt.[20]

It was in one of the palatial villas of Jericho that Zacchaeus entertained Jesus. Because of the wealth of Jericho, Zacchaeus must have been among the wealthiest of the tax collectors in Palestine.

From Jericho, which is 800 feet below sea level, Jesus and other Jewish pilgrims had to climb up to Jerusalem some 2500 feet above sea level in 12 miles. It was along this steep road that the victim in the story of the Good Samaritan (Luke 10:30) was waylaid by robbers. From New Testament Jericho if one travels up the Wadi Qelt he can see traces of an old Roman road. This road and most of the other Roman roads in Palestine date to the period after A.D. 70 when the Romans built them for the use of their legions. This would mean that Jesus and His disciples had to trudge along dusty dirt roads.

As Jesus approached Jerusalem he would come to the town of Bethany on the east slope of the Mount of Olives. The village is today called El Azariyeh in memory of Lazarus. The traditional tomb of Lazarus was mentioned by the Pilgrim of Bordeaux (A.D. 333). Steps were cut into the rock

12. The Church of the Holy Sepulcher.

in the seventeenth century to allow pilgrims to descend into the tomb. Excavations which were conducted under S. J. Saller from 1949 to 1953 showed that a church had been built near the tomb *c.* A.D. 390.

The traditional site of the Last Supper, the second-story room of the Cenacle, is but a reconstruction by the Franciscans of the fourteenth century. Below in the same building is the so-called "Tomb of David," revered by orthodox Jews. A stairway descending from "Mount Zion" to the Kidron Valley has been uncovered on the grounds of the Church of St. Peter Gallicantu ("of the crowing cock"). This may have been used by Jesus. The Assumptionist Fathers believe that their Church of St. Peter Gallicantu is the site of the Palace of Caiaphas, the high priest. Most Catholic scholars would favor a site farther up "Mount Zion" near the Cenacle complex. The traditional site of the House of Annas is in the Armenian Quarter within the walled city of Jerusalem. This goes back, however, only to a tradition of the fourteenth century.

The trial of Jesus took place in the *praetorium* or residence of Pilate in Jerusalem. Some scholars would identify this with Herod's palace at the Citadel area, the western entrance to the walled city of Jerusalem. The other and probably more plausible site is the Fortress Antonia, built by Herod and named in honor of his friend Mark Antony. The fort, which was about 500 feet long and 250 feet wide, with four towers seventy-five feet high, overlooked the temple area from the northwest. It was here that the Romans housed a cohort of 600 soldiers.

In 1856 Father Alphonse Ratisbonne bought the area near the so-called "Ecce Homo" arch for the Sisters of Zion, because since the Middle Ages this was believed to be the place where Pilate said, "Behold the Man." Later investigations, however, showed that the arch was part of Hadrian's triple arch dated to A.D. 135. But excavations in the 1930's by Hugues Vincent under the building of the Sisters of Zion have uncovered one of the most important structures of the New Testament age—the remains of the Antonia. The excavators found huge striated flagstones which were part of the courtyard. On the flagstones were games carved out by the Roman soldiers to while away their time; one of these may have been involved in the mocking of Jesus as a king. Knuckle-bones used as dice were also found. The description

13. Ossuaries from Dominus Flevit on the Mount of Olives.

of the *Lithostroton* or "Pavement" in John 19:13 as the scene of the trial of Jesus before Pilate accords very well with the huge flagstones of the Antonia.

In 1968 Israeli archaeologists discovered the first indisputable physical evidence of a victim of crucifixion. While clearing ground for apartments in northeastern Jerusalem at Giveat ha-Mivtar, builders found a number of cave tombs containing ossuaries with redeposited bones.[21] One of the ossuaries contained the bones of an adult male and a child. It was inscribed in Aramaic with the name *Yhwḥnn* or Yehohanan. The young man's *calcanei* or heel bones were still pierced by an iron nail; his calf bones had been broken. A careful study of the bones by N. Haas has yielded the following conclusions:

The whole of our interpretation concerning the position of the body on the cross may be described briefly as follows: the feet were joined almost parallel, both transfixed by the same nail at the heels, with the legs adjacent; the knees were doubled, the right one overlapping the left; the trunk was contorted; the upper limbs were stretched out, each stabbed by a nail in the forearm.[22]

The crucifixion may have taken place during the census revolt led by Judas of Galilee in A.D. 6–7 or at some time before the outbreak of the Jewish revolt in A.D. 66. After the latter date there would have been no opportunity for the Jews to have carefully reburied the bones in an ossuary. The new evidence is a vivid reminder of the brutality of crucifixion.

There are two sites which are pointed out as the location of Calvary (Golgotha) and the Tomb of Jesus: 1) Gordon's Calvary and the Garden Tomb favored by Protestants; 2) the Church of the Holy Sepulcher venerated by all other denominations.

It was in 1883 that General Gordon, who was to die at Khartoum two years later, visited Palestine. As a devout

14. The Roman Agora at Athens with the Tower of the Winds.

Christian he was interested in biblical topography. For the site of Calvary he chose a hill, which now bears his name, 150 yards north of the present walled city. What actually convinced Gordon was the fact that if one pictured ancient Jerusalem as a skeleton with its feet at the pool of Siloam, its head would lie to the north! Even before Gordon, in 1842 Otto Thenius, a German pastor, had been attracted to the same hill by two cavities which give it the appearance of a skull. A drawing made of the area by a traveler of the seventeenth century shows, however, that the two "eye-sockets" of Gordon's Calvary had not yet been formed at that time.[23]

The nearby "Garden Tomb," although it has been made a restful oasis for meditation, likewise has no claim to authenticity. Sockets for bolts and hinges in the jambs indicate that it was closed by a door and not a rolling stone. The so-called "window" is the top of the doorway of the originally independent chamber which has been partially blocked up with masonry. The tomb is probably of a Byzantine date.

On the other hand, the traditional site of the Church of the Holy Sepulcher as the location both of Calvary and of the Lord's tomb has much in favor of its authenticity. We know that the site of Calvary and other areas sacred to Christians were deliberately desecrated by the emperor Hadrian in A.D. 135. The Forum was laid over the area of Calvary, and dedicated to Venus. It was with the conversion of Constantine to Christianity that the pagan shrines were replaced at many sites with Christian edifices. In 326 the emperor ordered a building constructed to commemorate the places of the death and the resurrection of Jesus. As the church was being constructed the Pilgrim of Bordeaux (333) saw the site of Calvary and the Holy Sepulcher about a stone's throw away. He was first to refer to Calvary as a "little hill" *monticulus*; the New Testament itself says nothing about Calvary as a hill.

As executions were held outside the city, it is a requirement of the authentic Calvary that it be located outside the walls of Jesus' day. Josephus in describing the seige of Jerusalem by Titus speaks of three northern walls. The *first* northern wall is believed to have run directly from the Citadel in the west to the temple area along the line of the modern David Street. The exact line of the *third* wall is a subject of much scholarly debate. But as this was built by Herod Agrippa I (A.D. 40–44) it does not concern the issue of the location of Calvary. It is the line of the *second* wall which is crucial. Unfortunately Josephus' description of this wall is not detailed enough. As the Church of the Holy Sepulcher is located in the northwest section of the present walled city, for it to be authentic the line of the second wall would have had to extend west from Antonia and then turn south to join the first wall before reaching the area of the Church. To some military experts such a course seemed unlikely.

Nonetheless recent excavations in the Church of the Holy Sepulcher itself and in the vicinity have indicated that such was the case. Just to the rear of the rotunda which was built over the supposed Tomb of Jesus is a Jewish grave, known as the "Tomb of Joseph of Arimathea." Tombs, like places of execution, are located outside city walls. In 1960–61, eleven shafts were sunk in the Church but none in the rotunda itself. The results showed that the area was an ancient quarry. The rocky eminence designated as Calvary, whose shape is obscured today by the superstructure of the Church, would have reached an elevation of about thirty-five feet above the quarry floor.[24]

In the recent expedition at Jerusalem under Kenyon from 1961–67, an area near the Church of the Holy Sepulcher was excavated in a vacant site in the Muristan district. Kenyon discovered deep layers of fill from the seventh century B.C. and the first century A.D. and also evidence of quarrying from this time. As quarries, like graves and places of execution were located outside the city walls, this indicates that the area was not within the walls until after the time of Hadrian. Kenyon concludes that there is little reason to doubt the authenticity of the traditional site of the Church of the Holy Sepulcher.[25] Conant, however, raises the possibility that quarrying activities after the time of Jesus may have obliterated the actual grave of Christ.[26]

The *arcosolium* or ledge type of grave must have been used for Jesus. Tombs which were closed with heavy disc-shaped stones rolling in a channel, like that used for Christ, may be seen at several places: 1) at the so-called "Tomb of the Kings," actually the tomb of Helen of Adiabene, north of the walled city of Jerusalem: 2) at the Hypogeum of the Herods near the YMCA and the King David Hotel in Jerusalem, which is possibly the tomb of Agrippa I; 3) at Abu Ghosh; and 4) at several other sites, all from the New Testament period.[27] Once such a stone had been rolled into place in its groove, it would have been impossible for anyone—even if he had somehow revived—to have removed the stone, unaided, from within.

C. Paul the Missionary

Many archaeological discoveries, including inscriptions, enable us to follow "the steps of Paul" on his career as a missionary. An important Greek inscription which may have belonged to the synagogue of the "Libertines"—i.e. freedmen or former slaves—mentioned in Acts 6:9 was found by Raymond Weill in his excavation of 1913–14 on the Ophel hill in Jerusalem. The text reads as follows:

> Theodotus the son of Vettenus, priest and ruler of the synagogue, son of a ruler of the synagogue, son's son of a ruler of the synagogue, built the synagogue for reading of the law and for teaching of the commandments, also the strangers' lodging and the chambers and the conveniences of waters for an inn for them that need it from abroad, of which (synagogue) his fathers and the elders and Simonides did lay the foundation.[28]

Many Jews taken into captivity to Rome by Pompey in 63 B.C. were later freed. Theodotus was evidently the descendant of such a slave who had been freed by a Roman master. He and his ancestors had been able to prosper to such a point that they could return to Palestine and build a synagogue and a caravansary for overseas Jews (cf. Acts 2). Although the mass of Jews in the Diaspora were generally lax in their observance of their religion in comparison to those in Palestine, this was not true of Diaspora Jews like Theodotus who were so zealous as to settle in Jerusalem. This explains why the Diaspora Jews such as Saul of Tarsus were so vehemently opposed to Stephen's preaching.

After Stephen's martyrdom we see Saul so intent on his errand to persecute Christians that, contrary to usual practice, he is found traveling at midday (Acts 26:13) on the road to Damascus. Following his dramatic conversion Saul, better known as Paul, began to preach to the Jews in Damascus but had to escape from them over the wall in a basket. The Jews secured the cooperation of Aretas, who guarded the gate (II Cor. 11:32). This was Aretas IV (9 B.C.—A.D. 40), the Nabataean king whose daughter was the wife of Herod Antipas before his adulterous union with Herodias. The Nabataeans were Hellenized Arabs who controlled a vast area from their capital at Petra in the south to the Euphrates.[29] When Paul went to Arabia (Gal. 1:17) after his conversion, this probably means some territory of the Nabataeans rather than the Arabian peninsula, he may not have gone there for solitude as is usually thought but rather to preach to the very Nabataeans who had cooperated with his foes.

The disciples were first called "Christians" in Antioch (Acts 11:26). This was not a compliment but a nickname. The Antiochians were famed in antiquity for their aptitude for ridicule. They are known to have insulted not only Apollonius of Tyana but even the emperor Julian (the Apostate). Unfortunately the excavations at Antioch have yielded almost nothing of the early Jewish or Christian communities since the early levels are below the water table.

Acts 12 mentions the persecution of the Christians by Herod (Agrippa I), grandson of Herod the Great, which resulted in the death of James the son of Zebedee. Agrippa I was a popular and vigorous monarch who reigned from A.D. 40 to 44 as Judea's first independent king since the Roman procurators had been installed in A.D. 6. The theater at Caesarea which was the scene of Agrippa's fatal stroke (Acts 12:23) was excavated in 1959–61 by an Italian expedition, headed by Antonio Frova.

It was Agrippa I who built the so-called "third" northern wall of Jerusalem. The identification of this wall has been one of the most vexing questions in the archaeology of Jerusalem. Some 400 meters north of the present wall of Jerusalem fragmentary remains of a wall built of reused colossal stones have been traced for a distance of 375 meters. Excavations conducted by E. L. Sukenik and L. A. Mayer in 1925–27 led them to believe that this was the third wall.[30] Other scholars, however, have identified the line of the present north wall with that of the third wall.[31] If we were to accept the Sukenik wall as Agrippa's north wall, this would mean that the size of Jerusalem tripled from the time of Herod the Great to that of his grandson, so that in the latter's day it reached an area of 450 acres and housed 120—to 150,000 persons.[32]

Agrippa's persecution failed to intimidate the church. When Barnabas and Paul returned from Jerusalem to Antioch, they were commissioned by the Christians there to set out on a missionary venture to Cyprus and to Asia Minor. Luke tells us that in Asia Minor Paul and Barnabas fled from Iconium south "unto Lystra and Derbe, cities of Lycaonia" (Acts 14:6). On the basis of classical texts which spoke of Iconium as also in Lycaonia, Luke was held to be mistaken. But a monument found by Ramsay indicated that this was not true of the period when Paul preached in this area. This instance and other details of accuracy convinced Ramsay of Luke's trustworthiness as a historian.[33] After the missionaries had healed a lame man the populace of Lystra worshiped Barnabas as Zeus and Paul as Hermes (Acts 14:12). Inscriptions with dedications to Zeus and to Hermes have been found in the vicinity of Lystra.

On Paul's second missionary journey he and his companions crossed over into Europe. He first preached at Philippi, a frontier town settled by Roman veterans. Luke's use of the Greek word *meris* in his description of Philippi (Acts 16:12) to mean a "region" was held to be an error until papyri from Egypt demonstrated that colonists from Macedonia idiomatically used the word with this meaning. Lydia, who was one of Paul's first converts at Philippi, must have been a wealthy woman as she was a seller of purple cloth, which only the wealthy could afford to buy.

Paul, Silas, and Timothy traveled from Philippi on the famous Via Egnatia nearly one hundred miles west to Thessalonica. Luke's accuracy is again attested when he speaks of the *politarchs* at Thessalonica (Acts 17:6), translated "the rulers of the city." As this term was not found in any classical author, Luke's use of the word was suspect. But the term has been found in at least seventeen inscriptions in the area of Thessalonica, including an inscription on the Roman arch called the Vardar Gate which was removed in 1876.

When Paul came to Athens he preached his famous "Mars Hill" or "Areopagus" sermon near the Acropolis. In his reference to an altar with an inscription "To AN UNKNOWN GOD" (Acts 17:23), he was not rebuking the Athenians for their superstition as the King James translation of verse 22 implies, but was commending them for their religious zeal which he desired to be directed to the true God. Pausanias, Philostratus, and Diogenes Laertes mention such anonymous altars. During times of calamity when every known god had been placated, offerings were then made to unknown gods who may have been overlooked.

Paul's ministry at Corinth has been richly illuminated by excavations which have turned up a number of relevant inscriptions. In the agora may be seen the *bema* or "judgment seat" before which Paul was tried (Acts 18:12–17). Paul's judge was Gallio, the brother of Seneca, the famous Stoic tutor of Nero. Fragments of a stone inscription bearing a rescript of the emperor Claudius were found at Delphi, referring to Gallio as the "Proconsul of Achaea"—the precise title which Luke was careful to use. As the inscription is dated to A.D. 51–53 we are thus able to date the time of Paul's visit to Corinth.

Near the theater at Corinth was found an inscription reading: *ERASTVS-PRO-AED-S-P-STRAVIT*, which represents the Latin *erastus pro aedilitate sua pecunia stravit*, meaning "Erastus in return for his aedileship laid the pavement at his own expense." The *aedile* was the commissioner of public works. It is quite probable that this is the same Erastus who became a Christian and Paul's co-worker (Acts

15. The "bema" or judgment seat, at Corinth before which Paul was tried. The Acro-Corinth in the background was the site of the temple of Aphrodite and its sacred prostitutes.

19:22). In Rom. 16:23 Paul calls him the *oikonomos*, the "treasurer" or "manager" of the city. He was an important exception to the rule that not many wise or mighty were called into the kingdom (I Cor. 1:26).

In 1898 at the foot of the monumental entrance to the agora a part of a lintel was found with a broken Greek inscription that can be restored: "[Syn]agogue of the [Hebr]ews." Deissmann dated this between 100 B.C. and A.D. 200 and suggested that it belonged to the synagogue where Paul preached (Acts 18:4). He also felt that the "miserable appearance of the inscription" was indicative of the low social level of the Jews of Corinth. W. A. McDonald, however, argues that the careless style of lettering dates the synagogue inscription to a period later than the time of Paul. If so, this later synagogue may have stood over the earlier building of Paul's day.

Paul's third mission was spent largely at Ephesus in western Asia Minor, a metropolis of 500,000 inhabitants. Here was located the Temple of Diana (Greek Artemis), one of the seven wonders of the world. The remains of the temple were found by a persistent English architect, John T. Wood, who spent seven years searching for the site. The building proved to be 343 feet long and 164 feet wide. The theater where the angry Ephesians met (Acts 19:29–31) to protest Paul's preaching could have held 25,000 persons.

It was especially the silversmiths (Acts 19:24 ff.) who were upset at the danger Paul represented to their business of making silver statues of Artemis. An inscription in Greek and Latin from the theater describes the dedication of a silver image of Artemis by a Roman official, Vibius Salutaris, "to be set up in the theater during a full session of the *ecclesia* (assembly)."[34] From about 150 B.C. the goddess is depicted with several rows of bulbous objects on her chest, usually interpreted as breasts. Such a marble statue was found by the excavations of the theater at Caesarea. A more recent interpretation of the round objects is that they are ostrich eggs, serving as symbols of fertility.[35]

During his ministry at Ephesus Paul must have contacted the highest levels of society as well as the lowest, for we read that "certain of the chief of Asia, which were his friends" (Acts 19:31) tried to dissuade Paul from going to the theater. These men were *Asiarchs*, provincial dignitaries who were chosen from the wealthiest and most aristocratic men of the province. Acts 19:35 includes two terms which have specialized meanings. The "townclerk" or *grammateus* who quieted the crowd was no mere flunky but the democratic city's executive officer. He reminded the Ephesians that their town was a *neokoros* or a "temple-keeper" (KJV "worshiper") of the great goddess. The Greek word literally means "temple sweeper" but came to have the honorific meaning of "warden." A Greek inscription describing Ephesus as a "temple warden" of Artemis confirms Luke's use of the term.

Elsewhere we find Luke consistently using the accurate titles for different situations. He correctly calls the governor of Cyprus a *proconsul* (Acts 13:7), Greek *anthupatos*, since after 22 B.C. Cyprus was a senatorial rather than an imperial province governed by a legate. He calls the chief official in Malta "the first man of the island" (Acts 28:7), a title confirmed in both Greek and Latin inscriptions for the Roman governor of that island. H. J. Cadbury has remarked:

> Just as you can test a man's knowledge of modern Oxford and Cambridge by his ability to name correctly the presiding officer of each college whether as Master, Principal, Provost, Warden, Rector, President or Dean . . . so one can test Luke's knowledge of municipal institutions in the Aegean cities. His language fully meets the test.[36]

When Paul returned to Jerusalem for the last time he precipitated a riot because the Jews believed that he had taken the Gentile Christian Trophimus into the inner area of the temple which was reserved for Jews alone (Acts 21:27–30). Philo tells us that this inner precinct was separated from the area open to the Gentiles by a stone balustrade about four feet high on which were placed at intervals warnings in Greek and in Latin that no non-Jews were permitted any farther. In 1871 a perfect Greek copy of the warning inscription was found by Clermont-Ganneau. In 1935, while widening the road outside St. Stephen's Gate, workers came upon a fragmentary Greek copy of the same inscription. The full Greek text reads: "Let no foreigner enter within the screen and enclosure surrounding the sanctuary. Whosoever is taken so doing will be the cause that death overtaketh him."[37] Paul was no doubt referring to this barrier when he wrote in Eph. 2:14 of the middle wall of partition between Jew and Gentile which had been broken down by Christ.

After Paul's arrest by soldiers from the Fortress Antonia, he was taken under guard to Caesarea where he was held first under Felix and then under Festus. In his description of Paul's appearance before Festus, Luke's use of the term *kyrios* or "lord" (Acts 25:26) was once questioned. But numerous inscriptions have turned up using this title for Nero, so that Deissmann could say: "The insignificant detail, questioned by various commentators, who, seated at their writing-tables in Tübingen or Berlin, vainly imagined that they knew the period better than St. Luke, now appears thoroughly credible."[38] Luke's scrupulous accuracy in describing Paul's appearances before various Roman magistrates has prompted Sherwin-White to say: "The accounts of these trials in Acts is so technically correct that Roman historians since Mommsen have often used them as the best illustration of Roman provincial jurisdiction in this particular period."[39]

D. The Early Church

The earliest archaeological evidence of Christianity in Palestine comes from the ossuaries—limestone boxes used for the redeposit of the bones of the dead. These ossuaries bear names written in Hebrew, Aramaic, and Greek—some of which are names common among the early disciples. However, since most of these names are also common among Jews in general, further evidence is needed to associate any given ossuary with Christianity. Accompanying the names are at times symbols which in some cases seem to indicate adherence to Christianity.

In 1873 a cave in Bethany yielded burials which included the names Mary, Martha, and Eleazar (Greek Lazarus). Since Martha was a rather rare name, it is possible, although by no means certain, that these are the same as the Lord's friends. An even rarer name is that of Sapphira (Acts 5). This name is not listed in the dictionaries. But Sukenik noted that it occurred in both Aramaic and Greek spellings in ossuaries from Jerusalem, one of which may have contained the bones of the wife of Ananias. A name which had been found only in the New Testament is the name Barsabbas (Acts 1:23). This name has now been found in an ossuary from Talpioth, a southern suburb of Jerusalem.

In 1953 excavations under B. Bagatti were conducted on the grounds of Dominus Flevit ("The Lord Wept") on the slopes of the Mount of Olives. More than forty inscriptions have been found on the ossuaries which date from the New Testament period. About the same number of inscriptions were in Aramaic and in Greek, together with a few in Hebrew. These included many of the same names as found among the early disciples: Mary (i. e. Miriam), Martha, Eleazar (Lazarus), Simeon (Simon), Jairus, John, Jonathan, Judas, Sapphira, and Yeshua (Jesus). Most of these are quite common names.

The discovery in 1931 of an ossuary with the name in Aramaic "Jesus, son of Joseph," created a sensation, until Sukenik—the greatest authority on such ossuaries—quickly denied that this had anything to do with the Jesus of the Gospels. Josephus, for example, mentions no less than twenty persons with the name Jesus. At least six ossuaries with the name Jesus are now known.

Two ossuary inscriptions from Talpioth, discovered in 1945, have been called the "earliest records of Christianity" by Sukenik.[40] The finds in the tomb, including pottery, lamps, and a coin of Agrippa I from the year A.D. 42-43 all indicate that the tomb belonged to the period before A.D. 50. Two ossuaries bear the interesting inscriptions in Greek: 1) written in charcoal on one are the words *IĒSOU IOU*; 2) incised on the other ossuary are the words *IĒSOU ALŌTH*. Sukenik concluded that these are not the names of the individuals whose bones were contained in the ossuaries as one would expect,[41] but that they are rather cries of lamentation addressed to Jesus by two early Christians. But this would seem to be an odd sentiment to be expressed by Christians. More credible is the interpretation of Gustafsson that these enigmatic graffiti represent a cry for help and a prayer for resurrection addressed to Jesus by two Christians.[42] In favor of the view that these are Christian burials is the presence in the same Talpioth chamber of an ossuary with the name Barsabbas, otherwise known only from the New Testament.[43]

Some of the ossuaries from Dominus Flevit bear cross signs, which may or may not indicate adherence to Christianity. What seems to be of more certain import are monograms on two ossuaries: on one is the monogram of the Greek letters Chi and Rho, standing probably for an abbreviation of "Christian," and on the other a monogram of the Greek letters Iota, Chi, and Beta, standing perhaps for Iēsous Christos Boēthia ("Help!").[44]

One of the Talpioth ossuaries has several crosses drawn on its sides. Since the cross or a large X sometimes appears on a purely Jewish ossuary, such as that of Nicanor, it cannot always be taken as a Christian symbol.[45] In the case of the Talpioth chamber, as other elements seem to indicate that this was a Christian burial this may indicate that the cross was used as a Christian symbol as early as the first century. Jothams-Rothschild found crosses in the tombs of the second-third century in the Sanhedria area, a northern suburb of Jerusalem. He believes that these are evidence that some of the members of the Jewish families who owned these tombs had turned to Christianity.[46]

Crosses found at Pompeii and Herculaneum, which were both destroyed by the famous eruption of Vesuvius in A.D. 79, have been interpreted as evidence of early Christianity in Italy. The cross in Herculaneum was the trace on a panel of stucco of a cruciform object that had been fastened by nails.[47] Below the cross was a wooden stand which may have served as an altar.

Two copies of a fascinating anagram from Pompeii have also been interpreted by some scholars as the composition of early Christians.[48] The anagram reads as follows:

```
R   O   T   A   S
O   P   E   R   A
T   E   N   E   T
A   R   E   P   O
S   A   T   O   R
```

Note that the horizontal and vertical palindrome, TENET,

forms a cross, and that the twenty-five letters can be used to spell twice the first two words of the Lord's Prayer in Latin, PATER NOSTER, together with A and O, the first and last letters of the Greek alphabet (Rev. 1:8, etc.).

```
                    A

                    P
                    A
                    T
                    E
                    R
        A PATERNOSTER O
                    O
                    S
                    T
                    E
                    R

                    O
```

The square was quite popular throughout the Middle Ages until the nineteenth century as a talisman against fire, tempest, theft, and sickness.[49]

Excavations at St. Peter's Church in the Vatican may take us back to the first century. Beginning in 1939 excavations were conducted beneath the altar area of the church; the official report of the excavators was published in 1951. A set of bones was produced in 1965, and in 1968 Pope Paul VI announced that he was convinced that these were the very bones of Peter.

Much controversy and some mystery have surrounded the investigations. What is certain is that an *aedicula* or memorial shrine has been uncovered which may be identified with the "trophy" of St. Peter mentioned by Gaius *c.* A.D. 200, and which had been set up *c.* A.D. 160.[50] The Pope's conviction concerning the alleged bones of Peter rests on the work of Margherita Guarducci, professor of Greek epigraphy at Rome.[51] Part of her evidence is based on her interpretation of the graffiti near the *aedicula* as a crypto-language used by the faithful, an analysis which other scholars have rejected. The circumstances which surrounded her obtaining the so-called "bones of Peter," which had eluded the official excavators, are judged suspicious by Snyder.[52] The latter concludes that the bones of Peter may very well have been at the Vatican, but doubts that they will ever be found. Cullmann concedes only that Peter's execution took place in the area of the Vatican, and asserts that the grave of Peter cannot be identified.[53]

The traditional burial place of Paul is at the Church of St. Paul's Outside-the-Walls on the Via Ostiense. We may have to be content with Paul's living example as no systematic effort has yet been made to recover his bones!

III

QUMRAN AND
THE ESSENES:
The Dead Sea Scrolls

How were the Dead Sea Scrolls discovered? What are they worth? How can they be dated? Was John the Baptist an Essene? Did the Qumran Teacher of Righteousness anticipate the crucifixion and the resurrection of Jesus?

A. Discoveries and Purchases

By far the most revolutionary discovery that has been made is that of the Dead Sea Scrolls. What enhances the value of these finds is the paucity of perishable records which had been found in the Holy Land heretofore. When the greatest discovery in Palestinian archaeology was made, it was made not by trained archaeologists but by members of the Ta'amireh Bedouins seeking a lost goat.

At the beginning of 1947 Muhammad adh-Dhib and two companions were herding their flocks near Wadi Qumran northwest of the Dead Sea. As Muhammad searched after a stray goat he discovered the entrance to a cave. Instead of any treasure they might have wished for, the Bedouins found a jar in which were some smelly parchments.

It was in November, 1947, that Professor E. Sukenik of

the Hebrew University learned about the scrolls. As Arab-Jewish tensions were building up, Sukenik conferred with his son Yigael Yadin about the wisdom of traveling the few miles to Bethlehem to investigate the report of the scrolls. At this point Yadin was torn by opposing interests:

> What was I to tell him? As a student of archaeology myself, I felt that an opportunity of acquiring such priceless documents could not be missed. On the other hand, as Chief of Operations of Haganah, I knew perfectly well the dangers my father would be risking in traveling to Arab Bethlehem. And as a son I was torn between both feelings. I tried to hedge, but before leaving, son and soldier won and I told him not to go. I bade him and my mother *shalom* and left for Tel-Aviv. Fortunately, my father disregarded my advice and next morning left for Bethlehem.[1]

Sukenik was able to purchase three of the original seven scrolls (the incomplete Isaiah Scroll, the War Scroll, and the Thanksgiving Hymns).

In February of 1948 some of the manuscripts were shown to John C. Trever of the American Schools of Oriental Research. Recognizing the similarity of the script to that of the ancient Nash Papyrus, Trever wrote to W. F. Albright for his opinion. Albright cabled back in March congratulating Trever on "the greatest manuscript discovery of modern times." It was not until April 11, 1948, that news of the discovery was released to the public. A month later Jewish-Arab hostilities erupted into a full-scale war.

Early in 1949 Metropolitan Samuel of the Syrian Orthodox Church, who had secured the other four scrolls (the complete Isaiah Scroll, the Manual of Discipline, the Habakkuk Commentary, and the Genesis Apocryphon), smuggled them out to the United States, where all except the tightly rolled Apocryphon Scroll were photographed by Yale University. The Metropolitan, who now resides in New Jersey, had difficulty in selling the manuscripts. He even advertised them for sale in the *Wall Street Journal*:

Biblical Manuscripts dating back to at least 200 B.C. are for sale. This would be an ideal gift to an educational or religious institution by an individual or group.[2]

By good fortune Yadin was in the United States at the time and knew the worth of these manuscripts. Through the generosity of Mr. Samuel Gottesman the price of $250,000 was raised. These scrolls together with the others purchased by Sukenik are now housed in the Shrine of the Book near the campus of the Hebrew University in Jerusalem.

When the Ta'amireh Bedouins realized the monetary value of the manuscripts they began to scour the area of Qumran for other finds. In 1952 they discovered Cave II close to Cave I, then also Cave VI. Their most important find was that of Cave IV, a mere one hundred yards from the ruins of the monastery of Qumran at the edge of the wadi (dry stream bed). It was embarrassing for the archaeologists who had been working at the excavations of the monastery (Khirbet Qumran) to learn of this discovery at their feet. The cave, which turned out to be the library of the monastery, was remembered by a Bedouin who had chased a wounded partridge into it some years before. Later in 1956 the Bedouins also discovered seven extensive manuscripts in Cave XI to the north.

The Bedouins sold their finds to the Jordanian Department of Antiquities at a rate of about $1.50 per square centimeter ($2^{1}/_2$ centimeters make an inch). The fragments from the "Wounded Partridge" Cave earned them about $90,000, and all told they have made close to a half million dollars.

Archaeologists have not been as successful as the Bedouins in sniffing out manuscripts, but they did discover a number of productive caves. In 1952 R. de Vaux led archaeologists in an exploration of 200 to 300 caves in the area. Cave III yielded the Copper Scroll; a Cave V was discovered near Cave IV. In 1955 Caves VII–X were found in the area of Khirbet Qumran.

B. Dating the Finds

Although a number of scholars were skeptical at first, today only S. Zeitlin of the Dropsie College for Hebrew and Cognate Learning in Philadelphia persists in doubting the early date of the Dead Sea Scrolls. The evidence of palaeography (the study of ancient scripts) dates the various manuscripts from 250 B.C. to A.D. 70. The palaeography of the sectarian documents in particular would date the founding of the Qumran community to about 150–100 B.C.[3] A radio-carbon analysis of cloth associated with the manuscripts yielded a date of A.D. 33 (later revised to 20 B.C.) plus or minus 200 years.

Excavations at Khirbet Qumran, a mile south of the initial find, proved that the main levels of the settlement dated from Hellenistic and Roman times. Although no manuscripts were found in the ruins, they are clearly linked to the caves by the same type of pottery. Finally, several hundred coins found in the excavations date the limits of the main period of occupation from 135 B.C. to A.D. 68.

C. Old Testament Manuscripts

Prior to the discovery of the Qumran manuscripts our oldest extant Old Testament texts were those known as the Masoretic Text dating from the tenth century A.D.[4] The greatest significance of the Dead Sea Scrolls lies in the recovery of Old Testament manuscripts about a thousand years earlier than our medieval copies. Of the 500 some MSS (manuscripts) recovered from Qumran, 175 or one-third are biblical. Of the Hebrew canon only Esther is not represented—no doubt as an accident of survival. The oldest text is an archaic Exodus fragment dated to 250 B.C. or even earlier.

The traditional Hebrew text of the Old Testament preserved in our medieval manuscripts is called the Masoretic Text (MT) after the editorial work of Jewish scribes known as Masoretes. They labored from the fifth to the ninth century, introducing vowels into the consonantal text and adding notes in the margins. We were not sure how accurate the work of the Masoretes and their predecessors was. Some scholars dated the origin of the MT to the editorial activities of rabbis in the second century A.D. Thanks to Qumran we know that the MT goes back to a Proto-Masoretic edition antedating the Christian era, and we are assured that this recension was copied with remarkable accuracy. This means that the consonantal text of the Hebrew Bible must be treated with respect and not freely emended.

Most of the biblical MSS from Qumran belong to the MT tradition. This is especially true of the Pentateuch and some of the Prophets. What effect the evidence of the complete Isaiah scroll (cited in the RSV as "one ancient MS") from Cave I has made may be seen by comparing the Revised Standard Version translated in 1952 with the King James Version. Only thirteen new readings were introduced, most of which had the support of some of the ancient versions. We may therefore conclude that though the Isaiah scroll from Qumran diverged considerably from the MT in spelling and grammar, it has not warranted any major changes in the substance of the text of Isaiah.

The Septuagint (LXX), the Greek translation of the Old Testament begun *c.* 250 B.C., ranks next to the MT in importance for the reconstruction of the Old Testament text. It was widely used in New Testament times, as may be seen from the fact that the majority of the 250 Old Testament citations in the New Testament are from this version. When the LXX diverged from the MT some scholars had assumed that the LXX translators had taken liberties with their texts. We now know from Qumran that many of these differences were due to the fact that the translators were following a somewhat different Hebrew text belonging to what we may call the Proto-Septuagint family. At Qumran we have Hebrew texts of Exodus, Numbers, Deuteronomy, Jeremiah, Samuel and Job of this type. From the analysis of the I Samuel materials from Cave IV we learn that the Qumran scrolls provide a fuller text than either the MT or the LXX, though it is closer to the latter. The LXX text of Jeremiah is one-eighth shorter than the MT and some of the materials are in a different order. Professor Cross, who is in charge of publishing the biblical materials from Cave IV, suggests that some of the plusses of the MT in Jeremiah may stem from expansionist tendencies.[5]

In addition to MT and LXX types of MSS there are a few examples of manuscripts which underly the Samaritan recension of the Pentateuch made in the second century B.C. Waltke points out that both the Proto-Samaritan and the Proto-Septuagint texts are derived ultimately from an Old Palestinian recension which goes back to at least the fifth century B.C.[6]

The Apocryphal works accepted in the Roman Catholic Bible as deutero-canonical, and the Pseudepigraphical works were both rejected from the canon by the Jews. Until recently these works were known to us only in Greek translations. Qumran has now given us the Hebrew and Aramaic originals of some of these works. The Genesis Apocryphon was one of the original seven documents from Cave I. It was not published until 1956, and then only in part because of its poor state of preservation. The Aramaic MS comments in a legendary vein on passages in Genesis. One section describes the beauty of Sarah in great detail.

D. Sectarian Documents

In addition to the known biblical and non-biblical works, Qumran produced works written by the Qumran Sect itself, almost all of which were hitherto unknown. One document which had been known since it was discovered in the Genizah (storeroom for old MSS) of a synagogue in Cairo in 1897 is the Damascus Document, sometimes known as the Zadokite Document. At least nine MSS of this work have now been found at Qumran. The Damascus Document gives us important information about the history of the Sect.

The Manual of Discipline was one of the seven documents from Cave I. This gives detailed instructions concerning the entrance requirements of the Sect. Another of the Cave I scrolls is the *Hodayot* or Thanksgiving Hymns. These include some thirty hymns probably composed by a single individual, perhaps the Teacher of Righteousness. Still another of the Cave I scrolls is The War Scroll, which describes the tactics and the equipment that the Sons of Light will use in defeating the Sons of Darkness.

Commentaries called *Pesharim* have been found on Psalm 37, Isaiah, Hosea, Micah, Nahum, Habakkuk, and Zephaniah. The Habakkuk Commentary, one of the original MSS from Cave I, gives us important details about the persecution of the Teacher of Righteousness by the Wicked Priest. The Nahum Commentary makes reference to historical persons of the second-first centuries B.C.

There are in addition to the major documents outlined above a number of miscellaneous works. These include *Mishmarot*, MSS describing the courses of the priests adjusted to the Sect's solar calendar. *Testimonia*, collections of Old Testament texts related to the Messiah, are similar to those which could have been used by New Testament writers as they include composite quotations of a type cited in the New Testament. A Messianic Horoscope and a Cryptic Document indicate that the Sectarians were not opposed to the astrology of their day.

In 1967 after the June War Yigael Yadin announced the acquisition of a remarkable Qumran document which he has called "The Temple Scroll."[7] Yadin does not reveal how he came to acquire the scroll, but only mentions that it had been atrociously kept by its possessor. The scroll is now the longest known from Qumran. It is over twenty-eight feet in length, which is longer than the complete Isaiah Scroll.

The scroll, which is yet to be published, deals with four subjects: 1) religious rules concerning ritual cleanness; 2) sacrifices and offerings; 3) statutes of the king and the army; and 4) a detailed description of the temple. One of the unique features is that, according to Yadin, the author seems to pass off the scroll as a divine decree from God. In matters of cleanness and uncleanness the new scroll takes a more stringent position than the Pharisaic Mishnah. The scroll gives detailed instructions as to the building of the temple, even including directions for the building of public toilets north of the temple area. As the details of the projected temple do not accord with those of Herod's temple, this is further evidence that the Sect had rejected the Jerusalem sanctuary.

A document which is probably not to be associated with the Qumran Sect is the unique Copper Scroll found in Cave III in 1952. The text tells about the location of fabulous amounts of gold and silver at sixty places. John Allegro, who believes that it is a map of the treasures which were taken from the temple by Zealots fleeing from the Romans, made a survey of the identifiable sites in 1960 without results.

Other scholars such as Milik and Cross regard the text as folkloristic.

E. Excavations at Khirbet Qumran

Khirbet Qumran, the ruins of the monastery, lies on a marl cliff about a mile south of Cave I and close to the shore of the Dead Sea. The ruins have been known for some time. In 1851 F. de Saulcy had mistakenly identified the site as Gomorrah. It was not until some years after the discovery of the MSS in the caves that excavations were conducted at Khirbet Qumran from 1951–56 under G. L. Harding and R. de Vaux. The excavators found that the major settlement which can be associated with the scrolls from the caves dates back to the time of Hyrcanus I (134–104 B.C.). There was a brief abandonment of the site after an earthquake in 31 B.C. The Romans captured the settlement in A.D. 68.

The main buildings occupy an area only eighty meters square. The most striking feature of Qumran is the number of cisterns and pools, some of which may have been used for the ritual immersions of the Sect.[8] The cisterns were supplied water by an open aqueduct from the mountain to the west. Pieces of furniture interpreted as either a table and bench or as a seat and footrest were found together with ink wells.[9] These came from a *scriptorium*, an upper room used for the copying of the MSS. The largest room, seventy-two feet by fifteen feet, served as the refrectory for the Sect's communal meals. Some two miles to the south, farm buildings were found at the spring of Ain Feshka on the shore of the Dead Sea.

It has been estimated that 200–400 persons lived at Qumran at one time. Most must have lived in huts or tents outside the buildings. A few evidently lived in nearby caves where signs of occupation have been found. Between the Khirbet and the Dead Sea is a sizeable cemetery. The main cemetery

16. The dining room at Qumran.

contains about 1,100 burials with about one hundred burials in the secondary cemeteries. The excavators investigated thirty-one graves in the main cemetery and thirteen in the other sections. In the initial investigations in addition to male skeletons, six female skeletons were found, all but one in the secondary cemeteries. More recently, however, excavators have reported the discovery of more female skeletons in the main cemetery itself.[10]

F. The Essene Identification of the Qumran Sect

The Qumran Sect has been identified with many groups including the Hasidim, the Pharisees, the Zealots, and the Jewish-Christian Ebionites. The most plausible identification is with the Essenes, a sect known from the writings of Josephus, Philo, and Pliny. The latter speaks of the Essenes' "city" in the wilderness between Jericho and Ein Gedi near the shore of the Dead Sea.

Both the Essenes and the Qumran sectarians were ascetic groups. Both had a probationary period for their initiates, ranked members, held property in common, practiced repeated immersions, partook of a common meal, refused the use of oil, held apart from the sacrifices of the temple, stressed God's predestination, and were intolerant of outsiders.

There are to be sure some differences. The Essenes seem to have been a celibate community. But women have been found in the Qumran cemeteries. They may, however, have been brought here for burial from the villages where some married Essenes lived according to Josephus. From the descriptions of the Essenes, scholars have considered them pacifists. But Yadin argues that this may have been true of wars in general and not of the eschatological conflict described in the War Scroll. Josephus tells of some Essenes who participated in the First Revolt against the Romans.

G. Implications for New Testament Studies

Since John the Baptist was ascetic and celibate, lived near Qumran, and practiced baptism, a number of scholars have suggested that he might even have been a member of the Qumran Sect. This would be a plausible theory to explain some of the parallels between Christianity and Qumran.[11] On the other hand, John's asceticism can be explained by the fact that he was a Nazarite. His baptism was a single initiatory rite unlike the repeated immersions of Qumran.

The finds from Qumran have had a great impact on the study of the Gospel of John. Before Qumran the closest parallels to John were from Hellenistic literature and the late Mandaean texts.[12] By virtue of the many parallels between

17. The cemetery at Qumran.

John and the Qumran texts, its claim to be a first century Palestinian document is strengthened, and arguments for a second century date weakened. According to Raymond E. Brown, "The abstract language, the dualism of light and darkness, and other features which once seemed to rule out Palestinian origin now help to confirm it."[13]

The communion of the Church has been compared with the communal meals of the Sect, as both have an eschatological perspective in anticipating the future banquet with the Messiah. The Qumran meals, however, were not sacramental; the elements partaken did not represent anything and certainly had no reference to the self-sacrifice of the Messiah. The community of goods practiced in the early Church (Acts 2–5) has been compared with the communalism of Qumran. After a two-year probationary period the Qumran initiate renounced all right to his goods which became community property. Those who lied in this matter would be subject to a year's excommunication and deprivation of one-fourth of their food allowance. Whereas the community of goods at Qumran was obligatory, the community of goods in the Church was a voluntary matter.

Of great significance for New Testament studies is the new light shed on the office and function of "bishops." Some scholars had argued that Luke's picture in Acts of a church governed by the apostles was anachronistic, and was based on the intrusion of later Hellenistic ideas of organization. The institution of "bishops" in the Pastoral Epistles was also urged as an argument for dating them to the second century. Now the community at Qumran had over the Assembly of all the mature members a presiding priest called a *mebaqqer* or "overseer." According to Albright:

As described, the functions and character of the *mebaqqer* are virtually identical with those of the Christian bishop of the second century, and of course with those of the *episkopos* ("bishop") of the

Pastoral Epistles. Thus the one principal concrete argument against the Pauline date has vanished.[14]

That is, since Qumran furnishes us with first century evidence for the office of a "bishop," the letters of I Timothy, II Timothy, and Titus may be dated to the first century.

Because of the lack of other parallels, scholars in the late nineteenth and the early twentieth century had sought parallels to the "mystery" of Paul's epistles in the pagan mysteries of Isis, of Dionysus, of Mithras, etc. Raymond Brown, utilizing the materials from Qumran, has shown that the Pauline concept of "mystery" is quite explicable from Semitic sources alone.[15]

Of major importance for understanding the Epistle to the Hebrews is a document from Cave XI which deals with the enigmatic figure of Melchizedek. This new text describes Melchizedek as a heavenly deliverer similar to the archangel Michael. This may help to explain why the author of Hebrews stresses not only Christ's superiority to the Aaronic priesthood but also to the angels (Heb. 1–2). Heb. 7:3 which speaks of Melchizedek without parentage is usually explained on the basis that his ancestors were not mentioned in Genesis 14, but may be now interpreted in the light that Melchizedek was regarded as a supra-human being. "It is no longer necessary to suppose that the conception of a heavenly high-priest in Hebrews was influenced by Hellenistic Jewish, gnostic and/or Philonic traditions."[16]

A work called "The Description of the New Jerusalem," represented by fragments from Caves II, IV, V, and XI recalls Ezekiel 40–48 and also anticipates passages in Revelation. Albright argues that the reminiscences of pre-Christian Jewish literature, specifically of Essene writings, are too numerous to permit a late date for the Apocalypse. He himself would favor a date about A.D. 68 for the book of Revelation.[17]

While the many parallels between the Scrolls and the New Testament are helpful in establishing the early date of the New Testament writings, it would be going beyond the evidence to believe that the parallels, such as in the book of Hebrews, mean that this was directed at former Essenes who had been converted to Christianity, or that the New Testament is dependent on the Scrolls.[18]

H. The Teacher of Righteousness and Jesus of Nazareth[19]

From time to time sensational claims that the Teacher of Righteousness of the Dead Sea Scrolls anticipated the crucifixion and resurrection of Jesus have received much notice in the press.

On May 26, 1950, Professor André Dupont-Sommer of the Sorbonne provoked a controversy in Europe by a lecture in which he claimed that the Teacher of Righteousness had probably been crucified, had been raised from the dead, and had appeared in judgment against the city of Jerusalem at the time of the Roman general Pompey's entrance in 63 B.C. Since the initial lecture, Dupont-Sommer has repeated this claim—albeit with modifications—in various articles and books. He has said, for example, that Jesus "appears in many respects as an astonishing reincarnation of the Teacher of Righteousness."[20]

Then in the May 14, 1955, issue of the *New Yorker*, the critic and journalist Edmund Wilson described the exciting story of the discovery of the Scrolls. By his best-seller, *The Scrolls from the Dead Sea* (1955), Mr. Wilson helped to attract national attention to the Scrolls. He suggested that Jesus may have spent some of his childhood years with the Essenes.

Soon thereafter in 1956 views similar to Dupont-Sommer's were aired in BBC broadcasts by John Marco Allegro of the University of Manchester. Allegro's statements carried weight as he was a member of the international team of eight scholars entrusted with the official publication of the Qumran materials. His remarks were promptly repudiated by five members of the team who were in Jerusalem at the time.[21]

In an article in a 1966 issue of *Harper's Magazine* Allegro makes a series of even less restrained allegations.[22] By linguistic legerdemain he asserts that the name "Jesus" itself means "Essene," and indeed "magician." According to Allegro the descriptions of Jesus' table companions, the "harlots" and the "publicans," disguise Essene titles. To merely list such fantastic suggestions is to refute them.[23] Allegro's attempts at archaeology are no less ill-inspired. Simply disregarding all of the archaeological and traditional evidence of the Tomb of Jesus, he makes the incredible suggestion that a porch south of the so-called "Tomb of Absalom" in the Kidron Valley is the Tomb of Jesus![24]

We may wonder how scholars who are competent in Semitic philology can arrive at such sweeping allegations. The lay public without a knowledge of languages may very well be bewildered. We may better understand on what fragile foundations and hypothetical scaffolding such elaborate edifices are erected if we carefully analyze the evidence which is used.

The Teacher of Righteousness was not strictly speaking the founder of the Sect, as he appeared some twenty years after the community had been groping "like the blind." He may possibly have been the author of the Thanksgiving Hymns, which give us our greatest insight into the Sect's views of sin and salvation. It is only the Habakkuk Commentary, the Commentary on Psalm 37, and the Damascus Document which give us any explicit information on this figure. We learn that he was a priest who was persecuted by the Wicked Priest, i.e. the corrupt high priest in Jerusalem. The Sect which seemed to have looked for two messiahs—a priestly messiah and a kingly messiah—did not consider the Teacher of Righteousness a messiah.

Scholars are widely divided as to the historic setting of the Teacher of Righteousness (TR) and the Wicked Priest (WP), as may be seen by the following review: 1) In the period 175–62 B.C. Rowley and Black would identify the TR with the Zadokite High Priest Onias III and the WP with the hellenizing Jason or his brother Menelaus. 2) In the period 152–34 B.C. Milik, Sutcliffe, de Vaux, Vermes, Bruce, and Cross would consider the TR some unknown person and the WP either Jonathan or his brother Simon.[25] 3) In the period 134–76 B.C. Allegro and Brownlee would consider the TR some unknown person and the WP Alexander Jannaeus. 4) In the period 75–63 B.C. Dupont-Sommer would consider Hyrcanus II as the WP. 5) At the time of the War with Rome in A.D. 66 Roth and Driver would identify the TR with the Zealot Menahem and the WP with Eleazar the son of Ananias the high priest.

Let us now examine two passages in particular which are used by Allegro and by Dupont-Sommer to support their comparison of the Teacher of Righteousness with Jesus of Nazareth. The first of these is the *Nahum Commentary* II:13b.

The explanation of this concerns the furious Young Lion [who . . . took ven]geance on those who seek smooth things—he who hanged living men [on wood . . . which was not] formerly [done] in Israel; but he who was hanged alive upon [the] wood . . . .[26] (Note: the items in brackets represent restorations of gaps.)

Allegro interprets the "Young Lion" as Alexander Jannaeus, which is a plausible suggestion. The reference to hanging probably refers to crucifixion. We know from Josephus that Jannaeus crucified 800 rebels. Although he is not even mentioned, Allegro concludes that the Teacher of Righteousness as the enemy of the Wicked High Priest must have been one of those crucified. Even this supposition rests on the unproven assumption that Jannaeus was the Wicked Priest. What makes this even more unlikely is the probability that "those who seek smooth things" were not the Essenes of Qumran, but rather the Pharisees who were the enemies of Jannaeus. Of Allegro's interpretation H. H. Rowley says:

> It would seem that there is too much inference and too little evidence. There is no evidence whatever that the Teacher of Righteousness was concerned in this incident at all, whether it had to do with Jannaeus or another. It would surely be passing strange for the crucifixion of the Teacher of Righteousness—which Allegro thinks to have been of comparable significance for the sect with the crucifixion of Jesus for Christians—to be unmentioned in the text which has with so much publicity been declared to record it.[27]

The passage which has been used by Dupont-Sommer to buttress his sensational claims is found in the *Habakkuk Commentary* XI:4–8.

> The explanation of this concerns the Wicked Priest who persecuted the Teacher of Righteousness, swallowing him up in the anger of his fury in his place of *exile*. But at the time of the feast of rest of the Day of Atonement *he appeared* before them to swallow them up and to cause them to stumble on the Day of Fasting, their Sabbath of rest.[28] (Italics ours.)

Originally Dupont-Sommer took the word rendered "exile" *glwtw* to mean "to strip" and associated this with crucifixion. Other scholars such as Burrows and Kuhn favored the meaning "exile," which he has adopted in his 1962 translation cited here. The crux of the passage is the word rendered "he appeared." Dupont-Sommer believes that the subject of the verb is the Teacher of Righteousness. Other scholars believe that this refers rather to the Wicked Priest.[29]

The verb may mean "to shine; to reveal oneself; and to appear." At first Dupont-Sommer maintained that the word bore supernatural connotations. "Thus the Teacher of Righteousness, shining with a divine light," was his early rendering. In other words, he believed that this referred to the resurrection of the Teacher of Righteousness, appearing in judgment upon Jerusalem at the time of Pompey's entrance in 63 B.C. He now concedes that: "The Hebrew verb used here may also be translated 'he revealed himself to them', with no supernatural implications."[30]

In review we may note the following: 1) It is certain that the Teacher of Righteousness was persecuted by the Wicked High Priest. 2) It is possible that he may have been crucified, although the texts do not indicate this. 3) Alleged allusions to a resurrection and return of the Teacher of Righteousness are based on forced interpretations, and have been rejected by most other scholars.[31]

In actuality the differences between the Teacher from Qumran and the Teacher from Nazareth are far more striking than any superficial similarities. Professor Brownlee lists ten such differences, which we may cite and amplify as follows:[32]

1. "Unlike Jesus, the Teacher of Righteousness was a confessed sinner who gratefully acknowledged his dependence upon the forgiving grace of God." This point and the following are based on the plausible ascription of the Thanksgiving Hymns to the Teacher of Righteousness.

2. "Unlike Jesus, he must suffer in order to be purified from sin."

3. "Unlike Jesus, the Essene Master founded a community vowing hatred toward its enemies." The injunction "to hate all the sons of darkness" has led some scholars to believe that Jesus may have had the Essenes in mind when He said, "You have heard that it was said, 'You shall love your neighbor and hate your enemy.'" (Matt. 5:43). This could be said of the Essenes but not of the Pharisees.

4. "Both teachers founded a church—but only Jesus built

a church which the powers of death could not overcome." After the destruction of their settlement by the Romans in A.D. 68 we hear no more about the members of the Qumran community.

5. "Unlike Jesus, the Teacher called his followers out of the world, but Christ on the contrary sent His followers into the world." The Sectarians were admonished to keep separate from non-believers and to conceal their doctrines from them.

6. "Unlike Jesus, the Teacher of Righteousness does not appear to have been 'a friend of publicans and sinners.'"

7. "Unlike Jesus, the Essene Master performed no works of healing, nor in other ways did he engage in acts of compassion among the needy." Indeed, in contrast to Jesus who welcomed the sick and deformed, the community excluded anyone with a physical defect: ". . . every (person) smitten in his flesh, paralyzed in his feet or hands, lame or blind or deaf, or dumb or smitten in his flesh with a blemish visible to the eye, or any aged person that totters and is unable to stand firm in the midst of the Congregation: let these persons not en[ter] . . . ."[33]

8. "Unlike Jesus, he was at most a prophet, not a redeemer."

9. "Unlike Jesus, the Teacher of Righteousness was simply preparing the way for one far greater than himself."

10. "Unlike Jesus, the Teacher of Righteousness founded a community enmeshed in legalism." The Essenes were so fanatical in their observance of ritual law that they considered the Pharisees to be lax. Since this was the case Stauffer says: "I contend: had Jesus fallen into the hands of the Wilderness sectarians, they would have murdered him as ruthlessly as did the Pharisees."[34]

IV

FRAGMENTS
AND CIRCLES:
The Nature of the Evidence

How much of the evidence has survived the ravages of time? How many of the ancient sites have archaeologists been able to excavate? When does the lack of evidence for a biblical statement prove that an error is involved? Does archaeology offset the negative appraisal of the Bible developed by higher criticism?

A. The Fragmentary Nature of the Evidence[1]

Historians of antiquity in using the archaeological evidence have very often failed to realize how slight is the evidence at our disposal. It would not be exaggerating to point out that what we have is but a fraction of a fraction of the possible evidence.

1. *The Fraction That Has Survived*

First of all, only a fraction of what is made or what is written ever survives. The Late Bronze city of Jericho seems to have been almost all but completely eroded by wind and rain over a period of four centuries of abandonment. Henri Frankfort estimated that nearly twenty feet had been eroded from the top of Tell Asmar (Eshnunna) in eastern Babylonia during two millennia.

In addition to the natural forces of erosion and decay, the agency of human depravation has been at work. The ruins of Babylon have been regularly mined by nearby residents and by those from as far away as Baghdad, fifty-four miles north. The stone structures of Caesarea have been re-used within the last 200 years in Acre, Jaffa, and even distant Venice. Champollion, who visited Sais in the Egyptian Delta in 1828, described extensive ruins. A century later in 1922 Henri Gauthier related that villagers had virtually denuded the site in their search for *sebakh*, the nitrogenous fertilizer formed by decaying mud bricks.[2]

Perishable materials such as papyri have completely disappeared from some sites. It is regrettable that no papyri have been found at Byblos in Phoenicia, as this is the port through which the Greeks imported Egyptian papyri and for which they named their books *biblos*. We know from clay sealings that papyri were used in the Aegean in the Minoan-Mycenaean period and in lower Mesopotamia in the Seleucid period, but none have been recovered.

In some areas even the more durable stone inscriptions seem not to have survived, or at least have not been recovered. It is reasonable to expect that the kings of Israel and Judah erected stone stelae similar to the Mesha Stone. But only one fragment of an Israelite stela containing a single word has been discovered. This was from Samaria and was published by Sukenik in 1936.

There were hundreds of synagogues in Palestine in the New Testament period. Only one synagogue from before A.D. 70 has been discovered—that at Masada. Inscriptions listing the twenty-four courses of the priesthood probably hung in hundreds of synagogues in Palestine. Thus far only fragments of two such inscriptions have been recovered—one found at Askalon in the 1920's, and fragments from Caesarea in the 1960's. In a fragment from Caesarea (dated to the third–fourth century A.D.) the name "Nazareth" appears. According to Avi-Yonah, "This is the only time so far that the name 'Nazareth' has been found in an inscription, in particular in a Hebrew inscription; it is also the earliest occurrence of the name in Hebrew."[3]

Even works of great literary merit which deserved to be carefully preserved have survived only in part. Of all the Greek lyric poets who wrote in the seventh and sixth centuries B.C. we have manuscripts only for Theognis and Pindar, and but fragments for the rest. Only about one-tenth of even the works of the three greatest Greek dramatists —Aeschylus, Euripides, and Sophocles—have come down to us. Menander, the most famous Hellenistic dramatist, wrote over one hundred plays. We have in hand only one complete play—discovered in 1955—and counting fragments, about five percent of his works.[4]

2. *The Fraction That Has Been Surveyed*

In the second place, only a fraction of the available sites have ever been surveyed. According to Samuel, "All in all, well over 300 Mycenaean sites are known, and it is probable that this number would be quadrupled if all Greece were carefully explored for evidence."[5]

Iraq, which comprises most of ancient Mesopotamia, is dotted with the ruins of ancient cities. Edward Chiera declared that he could not find a place in the land of Iraq, except in the newly formed delta, from which one could not see two or three mounds. Yet Robert Adams reported recently: "Even the best maps of Iraq record only a minute and capricious fraction of the ancient mounds or *tells* with which particularly its southern plains seem to be covered almost continuously."[6]

In 1944 the Palestine Gazette listed a total of about 3,000 sites in Cis-Jordan (the area west of the Jordan River), and several hundred in Trans-Jordan. By 1963 the total of known sites had increased to about 5,000 largely as a result of the surveys by Nelson Glueck. In 1966–67 surveys by Beno Rothenberg in the Negeb and the Arabah turned up more than 200 new sites; Rothenberg's survey of the Sinai in 1968 discovered more than one hundred previously recorded sites.

The Israeli surveys of 1967–68 in the occupied Golan Heights, Samaria, and Judah have substantially increased the total. Dr. Moshe Kochavi, the director of the Judean survey writes: "Our Survey surveyed about 1,200 sites, of which some twenty to thirty percent are new sites previously unrecorded. . . . I estimate that not more than one-third of the amount of possible sites were recorded, and a thorough survey is a question of many years (including the yet unsurveyed parts of pre-war Israel)."[7] All told, close to 2,000 sites were examined by the Israeli teams, of which about 800 were previously unknown.

3. *The Fraction That Has Been Excavated*

In the third place, only a fraction of the surveyed sites have been excavated. In 1963 Paul Lapp estimated that of 5,000 sites in Palestine there had been scientific excavations at about 150 sites, including twenty-six major excavations. He qualified this statement by noting: "To be sure, many of the sites on record would not merit extensive excavation, but if only one in four were promising, major excavations have till now been carried out at only two percent of the potential sites."[8] Since 1963 additional excavations have been undertaken, but since over a thousand new sites have been added to the total by the recent surveys, the actual percentage of sites excavated has not increased but decreased.

Seton Lloyd notes that by 1949 more than 5,000 mounds

had been located in Iraq.[9] As of 1962 Beek's atlas recorded twenty-eight major excavations in Iraq, less than one percent of the total sites.[10] When Leonard Woolley wished to excavate in the Amuq Plain at the mouth of the Orontes River in Syria he had to choose from among 200 unexcavated mounds which dot that plain.[11]

Excavations in Egypt have been concentrated on the tombs and temples of Upper Egypt along the dry, southern area. Humidity and ground water have deterred excavations at all but a few sites in the Delta area of Lower Egypt. Memphis, the capital of the Old Kingdom, is yet to be excavated.

Many ancient sites are still occupied so that their excavation is impossible or impractical. At the turn of the century it was possible to move an entire village from an ancient settlement, as at Delphi in Greece. Today to excavate the important but occupied site of Thebes in Greece would require close to a million dollars for the expropriation of the land according to the Greek Inspector General of Antiquities.[12]

It is for the same reason that excavations are out of the question at Arbela-Erbil in Mesopotamia. With the exception of a salvage operation, one of the two mounds of Nineveh, Nebi Yunus, has not been excavated because it is the site of a modern village and cemetery. Madhloum, who has been conducting some work in other areas of Nineveh, speaks of all the previous work that has been done there as "no more than scratches applied to an enormous body."[13] The important Assyrian city of Arrapkha (Kirkuk) has not been excavated. Damascus in Syria, and the Phoenician cities of Sidon and Tyre are still occupied. Since 1947 excavations of a section of Tyre have yielded Byzantine and Roman levels. But sad to say there has been almost no excavation in Iron Age levels of any Phoenician town.[14]

In Anatolia a number of New Testament sites are still unexcavated. The site of Thyatira is occupied by the modern town of Ak-Hissar, that of Philadelphia by Alah-Shehir, and that of Iconium by Konya, so that excavations here are not likely. But Lystra remains to be excavated as does the site of Derbe, which was identified only in 1964. Within a sixty-mile radius of Smyrna-Izmir, twenty-five ancient cities lie exposed to the elements and untouched by the archaeologist's spade.

In Israel apart from occupied sites such as Gaza and Nebi Samwil, many unencumbered mounds still remain unexcavated, e.g. Phasaelis, Jezreel, Tell Akko, Khirbet Muqaneh (possibly Ekron), etc. The last two tells are so extensive that thorough excavations could cost a million dollars.

4. *The Fraction That Has Been Examined*

In the fourth place, with the exception of small and short-lived sites such as Tell en-Nasbeh, Qumran, and Masada, it is always the case that only a fraction of any excavated site is actually examined. The wealthy Oriental Institute excavations at Megiddo from 1925–34 succeeded in completely removing the top four strata. But this grandiose scheme was abandoned in later seasons and has not been attempted at any site of comparable size. Since only a fraction is examined, this means that any given excavation may very well miss important finds.

The British excavated at Zakro in eastern Crete in 1901. They found houses but missed a palace, which was not found until excavations were resumed in 1962. At Ephesus since 1894 the Austrians have found vast remains of the later periods. But nothing of the Bronze Age came to light until 1963 when Turkish engineers built a parking lot and found a Mycenaean burial. For decades nothing of the Bronze Age was found at Halicarnassus, until in 1962 George Bass saw a man walking down the street carrying a Mycenaean jar from a nearby village.[15]

The Iraqi excavations at Eridu, the seat of Enki (the god of wisdom), did not produce a single tablet. Even at Calah-Nimrud, which was the second major site to be explored in the Near East and which was subject to several excavations in the nineteenth century, the re-excavations by Mallowan (1949–63) have been able to produce spectacular finds. In all of the pre-Mallowan expeditions only two cuneiform tablets had ever been found; numerous tablets were recovered by the recent expedition.

As indicated in our discussion of the Conquest, the lack of significant Late Bronze remains at Jericho, Gibeon, and Ai poses a difficult problem. The lack, however, may not necessarily mean the inaccuracy of the biblical account, but simply the incompleteness of the archaeological excavations. There are, for example, no early Iron age cemeteries discovered for Samaria, Jerusalem, Shechem, Beth Shan, Tell en-Nasbeh, Tell Beit Mirsim, or Megiddo, though we know that these sites were occupied in the early Iron Age.[16] The Mazar excavations at En-Gedi from 1962–64 failed to turn up any remains from the second century A.D., yet we know that there was a settlement there at that time from the Bar Kochba letters.

From soundings made at Hazor in 1928 Garstang concluded that the site was not an important city in the fourteenth and thirteenth century B.C. because of the complete lack of Mycenaean imports. Yet Yadin in his recent excavations found floors littered with Mycenaean pottery. The site of Hazor is comprised of an upper city of thirty acres and a lower city of 175 acres. Working with an unusually large staff of over thirty archaeologists and a crew of over a hundred laborers, Yadin managed to clear one-four hundredth of the site in four seasons from 1955–58. "He has suggested that it would take 800 years of about four or five months work (Yadin's season was three months) per year to clear the entire site."[17]

To be sure Hazor is unusually large for Palestine. About the only comparable site is Ashdod, which is now believed to have covered 175 acres. Other Old Testament sites are considerably smaller, ranging in acres as follows: Gezer and Tell el-Ajjul, thirty; Ai, twenty-seven and a half; Dothan and Arad, twenty-five; Lachish, eighteen; Gibeon, sixteen; Ashkelon, fifteen; Megiddo, thirteen; Tell Beit Mirsim, seven and a half; and Jericho, seven. But some sites in the Near East are even larger than Hazor. Oppenheim lists their sizes as follows:

> The largest city was undoubtedly Babylon in the Chaldean period; its area covered 2,500 acres. Then follows Nineveh, with 1,850 acres, while Uruk was somewhat smaller, with 1,100 acres. Other cities are much smaller: Hattusha, the Hittite capital, occupied 450 acres; Assur had only 150 acres. Among the royal cities, Dur-Sharrukin was 600 acres, Calah, 800 acres.[18]

Campbell Thompson estimated that with a force of a thousand men, each shifting 120,000 tons a year, to remove the 14,500,000 tons of earth represented by Quyundjik—one of the mounds of Nineveh—would take 124 years. But at Yadin's estimated rate of progress for Hazor, to completely excavate Babylon would take 8,000 years!

In view of the fractional nature of almost all excavations, Paul Lapp issues the following warning:

> With such limited and uncontrolled sampling, negative conclusions are always dangerous. At one site, for example, we excavated two squares to bedrock, but only subsequently did we find evidence of occupation in the Chalcolithic and Early Bronze periods. Even after excavating a fairly large quarter of the town, we have no clear

evidence of what is known, from literary sources, to be one of the town's flourishing periods. Statements like, "There was no Bronze age occupation at this site," "This area was not occupied in the Iron age," and "There was no sedentary occupation in Palestine in Middle Bronze I," must always be accepted with considerable reservation because of the limited sample of evidence upon which they are based.[19]

5. *The Fraction That Has Been Published*

In the fifth place, only a fraction of the materials, and especially the inscriptions in languages other than Greek and Latin, produced by excavations has as yet been published.[20] Because of the relative scarcity of scholars who can publish inscriptions in cuneiform and other types of scripts, there is often a serious time lag between the acquisition of texts and their publication.

A Babylonian king list acquired in the 1880's by the British Museum was published in 1954. The Berlin Coptic Codex acquired in 1896 was not fully published until 1955. Tablets of the Lipit-Ishtar Code excavated at Nippur by the University of Pennsylvania at the end of the nineteenth century lay on the shelves of the University Museum in Philadelphia until their significance was recognized by Francis Steele, who published them in 1947. Erle Leichty, Curator of Akkadian Language at the University Museum explains:

> With few exceptions, western museums have still not caught up with the flow of antiquities and their basements and storerooms are full of undiscovered treasures.
>
> In the field of Assyriology, of course, we rely almost entirely on existing collections of cuneiform tablets rather than on new excavations. We have absorbed such a small percentage of the hundreds of thousands of tablets in museums that new discoveries are almost routine. In a tablet collection the size of the one at the University Museum every drawer holds a surprise. The only problem we have is which drawer to open . . . .[21]

Nippur was the earliest site to be excavated by the Americans (1889–1900). To a large extent the Sumerian texts from Nippur recovered by the early expedition have been published, though many unpublished texts remain. But few of the texts from the current University of Chicago excavations since 1948 at Nippur have been published. More than 16,000 cuneiform texts have come from Kanish (Kultepe) in eastern Turkey since 1882. Of these texts from the Old Assyrian period, about 2,000 have been published. "The main body of texts, excavated by the Turkish Historical Society since 1948, has remained unpublished but for a handful of tablets and is not accessible to scholars."[22]

Of the 25,000 cuneiform documents found at Mari, about 2,800 have now been published. Of the Assyrian letters found at Nineveh about 2,000 are still unpublished in the British Museum. The main bulk of the tablets excavated by the University of Chicago from 1930–36 at Tell Asmar (Eshnunna) remains unpublished. Many of the texts found at Adab from 1903–1904 are unpublished, as are many texts from Babylon. Of the total of 500,000 cuneiform documents thus far recovered, Samuel Kramer estimates that but ten percent have been published.

As opposed to the tentative, preliminary reports published year by year in journals, the final, comprehensive reports of excavations, including detailed illustrations of objects found, drawings of sections and plans, etc. are often delayed for many years. Such publications are time consuming to write up and expensive to publish. Indeed the wealth of materials excavated demands more time for careful study and publication than the relatively simple task of removing the objects from the earth.

The most spectacular discovery in Egyptian archaeology was that of the unlooted tomb of Tutankhamon by Howard Carter in 1922. It took almost six full years to empty the tomb of all its precious objects, and ten years before the completion of the first general publication. Speaking of King Tut's tomb, Alan Gardiner has said:

Yet the sad fact is that the results have never been properly published in the scientific sense; that is, with a detailed description of *every* object found, illustrated by colored plates. In 1926 Carter told me he estimated that such a publication would cost £30,000. Today (1961) it would cost little short of £100,000.[23]

The excavations at Baalbek from 1899–1904 were finally published in 1925. The results of the 1900–1909 excavations at Phaistos on Crete were not fully published until 1951. The excavations at Ur by Woolley were completed in 1934. Volume VIII of the *Ur Excavations* appeared in 1965; as yet the volume on the Ur III and Larsa periods has not appeared. The excavations at Beth-shan, which were completed in 1933, have not been fully published, though a volume on the Iron Age levels by F. W. James did appear in 1966.[24]

Speaking of the complete publication of what is already available, Albright has said: "At the present rate, one may estimate roughly that it will be fifty years before the material already accessible has been adequately published.[25] Of course, by that time we shall have as much if not more of new, unpublished materials.

Now if one could by an optimistic estimate reckon that one-tenth of our materials and inscriptions has survived, that six-tenths of the available sites have been surveyed, that one-fiftieth of these sites have been excavated, that one-tenth of the excavated sites have been examined, and that one-half of the materials and inscriptions excavated have been published, one would have ($1/10 \times 6/10 \times 1/50 \times 1/10 \times 1/2$) at hand but six, one hundred-thousandths of all the possible evidence.[26] This estimate must take into account the factor of redundancy. That is, in cases of mass-produced items such as pottery one does not have to discover many examples of the same type of pot to set up a corpus of representative types. On the other hand, this fraction becomes significant when considering the paucity of relatively rare items, such as historical inscriptions.

Coins, for example, were minted in quantities. Yet an examination of any numismatic catalogue will show numerous examples of unique specimens; that is, only one out of the hundreds or thousands has been found in these cases. There were 116 Assyrian kings, not a few of whom probably erected more than one statue of themselves. Yet statues in the round of only two kings, Shalmaneser III and Ashurnasirpal II, have been discovered.

Every temple in Egypt had papyri records describing its personnel and their tasks month by month. From a small temple at Abusir we know that it would have taken ten meters of papyri per month or 120 meters (about 130 feet) per year to list such records. If we were to estimate that there were only one hundred temples in Egypt, and were to multiply this times the 2,000 year period from 2500–500 B.C., we could calculate (120 × 100 × 2,000) that the Egyptians must have used a total of 24 million meters of papyri for their temple records. Of this grand total the only temple records that have been recovered are thirteen meters from Abusir and a similar length from Ilahun.[27] An even more striking example of the small fraction of our survival and recovery of texts is given by Samuel:

> In the first 300 years of the empire there were never less than twenty-five Roman legions, and each legion had 5000 men. The legions were paid three times a year, so that there were 375,000 pay vouchers a year. Multiply that by 300, and the result is 112.5 million. Of those, only six and a fragment of a seventh survive.[28]

B. Overlapping Circles of Evidence

The sources at our disposal for the reconstruction of ancient history may be divided into traditional and non-traditional sources. Traditions, such as those incorporated in Homer, Herodotus, and the Old Testament, have been transmitted either orally or in written manuscripts from generation to generation. Professional historians have been accustomed to look at these traditions with a skeptical eye wherever these have lacked corroborative external evidence. The latter consists of non-traditional or contemporary evidence which may be divided into two categories: 1) material remains; and 2) inscriptional evidence. The first category could also include a sub-category of artistic evidence for areas such as Greece. But for Israelite history such evidence is scanty. Inscriptional or epigraphical evidence would include such documents as royal inscriptions, letters, treaties, contracts, etc., of which relatively few have been found in Palestine.

If one plotted the sources of our evidence for ancient history as overlapping circles, one could see that there are theoretically seven possible combinations: three in which one source stands alone, three in which two sources overlap, and an ideal situation in which the three sources overlap.

That each of these situations may occur may be seen from

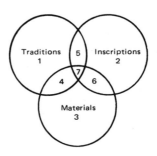

a chart of the evidence for plants and animals prepared by Emily Vermeule, *Greece in the Bronze Age* (1964). In her list inscriptions are represented by Linear B texts, and tradition by Homer. 1) The apple is attested alone in Homer; 2) the mint alone in Linear B; 3) the almond alone by excavations; 4) the pear by both Homer and excavations; 5) the cypress by both Homer and Linear B; 6) the coriander by both Linear B and excavations; and 7) linen by all three sources.

The implication of this random distribution is that just as an object may be attested alone by excavations or alone by inscriptions, it may very often stand alone in the traditions without any necessary reflection upon its authenticity. Yet scholars have often worked under the assumption that the overlap of traditions with either inscriptional or material evidence is not only desirable but necessary.

It is often assumed that the historicity of a person is suspect unless corroborated by inscriptional evidence, e.g. Darius the Mede in the book of Daniel. Attempts to identify a person in the traditions with someone in the inscriptions may founder on the lack of overlapping evidence. Before cuneiform documents were discovered that identified Belshazzar as the son of Nabonidus, some declared his name a pure invention, and others tried to identify him with Evil-Merodach or Neriglissar.[29] Tatnai (Ezra 5:3, 6) was mistakenly identified with the satrap over Babylon, Ushtannu, until Olmstead in 1944 called attention to a text where *Ta-at-tan-ni* is mentioned as a governor subordinate to the satrap.[30]

If we had to depend upon inscriptional evidence to prove the historicity of Pontius Pilate, we would have had to wait until 1961, when the first epigraphical documentation concerning him was discovered at Caesarea.[31] The first epigraphical attestation of Herod the Great was discovered in the 1963–65 expedition to Masada.[32] In 1966 the first inscriptional reference to Felix the procurator was found ten miles north of Caesarea.[33]

At times when secular inscriptions and biblical traditions do overlap there are discrepancies between the two sources. We cannot assume that in these cases the secular inscriptions are correct and that the Bible is in error simply because the former are contemporary and the latter is a traditional source. Particularly in royal inscriptions we must take into account distortions introduced by a king's vanity. We have both Egyptian and Hittite accounts of the battle of Kadesh fought in the reign of Ramesses II. According to the Egyptian account Ramesses won a great victory; he was in fact fortunate to have escaped with his life. Sargon II claimed credit for the capture of Samaria, whereas the biblical account (II Kings 17:6, 18:10) suggests that it was his predecessor Shalmaneser who was responsible. The Bible is correct as the city fell in August/September 722 B.C., and Shalmaneser died in December.[34]

All of these examples indicate that in view of the fragmentary nature of the non-traditional material and inscriptional evidence—evidence which is partial and fortuitous in survival and exiguous in recovery—and in view of the nature of the overlapping circles of evidence, one cannot demand the complete corroboration of elements in the traditions by archaeological data.

C. The Argument from Silence

Unfortunately many scholars who seem not to be aware of these factors of the "fragments" and "circles" of the archaeological evidence have used the argument from silence in criticizing the traditions, whether classical or biblical. That is, any element in the traditions which was not corroborated by archaeological evidence has been considered suspect or anachronistic.

For example, Homer constantly refers to the bronze greaves and corslets (breastplates) of his heroes. H. L. Lorimer in 1950 wished to delete the lines that mentioned bronze corslets as late interpolations, because no known corslets of an early date had been discovered.[35] In 1960 at Dendra in Greece the first known metal corslet of the Bronze Age was discovered.[36] Then three years later a second bronze corslet was found.

In 1948 George Hanfmann denied that there was any evidence for a major Greek migration to Ionia before the eighth century B.C. as claimed in Greek traditions.[37] Writing in 1965 he indicates that we now have ample evidence from pottery confirming the tradition of an eleventh century migration.[38]

Roman historians of the nineteenth century questioned the traditions of the early foundations of Rome. Then in 1948 foundations of pre-Roman huts were found on the Palatine Hill, and pre-Roman tombs were found in the Forum. According to Picard: "The material contained in these tombs and in the huts can be dated in relation to that found on other sites: it seems most probable that it goes back to the middle of the eighth century B.C., i.e., the very period when, according to tradition, Romulus and Remus settled on the Palatine."[39]

The Bible (Lev. 18:21; II Kings 23:10; Jer. 7:30–31) repeatedly denounces the horrible practice of sacrificing children to Moloch practiced by the Canaanites and Phoenicians. "In spite of the documentation available in pagan and Christian sources about human sacrifice in Phoenicia and Carthage," Albright informs us, "the rationalistic critics of the nineteenth and early twentieth centuries refused to believe that the reports had any basis, especially since archaeological work seemed not to furnish any support."[40] Discoveries in cemeteries in Carthage, the colony of Phoenicia, have now bared grim evidence of the custom of burning babies on pyres.

These examples of the criticism of traditions on the basis of arguments from silence and of the recent corroboration by archaeology of these suspect traditions—as they are drawn from the classical world—indicate that the archaeological confirmation of the Bible is not an isolated phenomenon concocted by theological apologists but is part of a larger development.

The negative judgments based on literary analysis and on lack of evidence are being generally replaced by a more positive appreciation for the traditions. Professor Avi-Yonah explains why we must be wary of drawing dogmatic negative conclusions from the lack of archaeological data at any given moment: "Archaeological evidence differs from literary sources in being continuously added to as research progresses. It is thus very dangerous to draw dogmatic conclusions from existing material or to argue *ex silentio*."[41]

In view of the fragmentary nature of the archaeological evidence, Roland de Vaux has issued the following warning about *ex silentio* arguments:

Finally, one must remember that the witness which archaeology and the texts afford is and always will remain incomplete. The earth's crust has preserved only a small portion of the monuments and objects of antiquity, and archaeology has recovered only a small proportion of these; also, those texts which we have represent only a very small part of that which was written, and even so would not represent everything necessary for the work of the historian. Thus archaeology can mitigate the silence of ancient texts to a certain degree, but *one must also admit that lack of archaeological evidence would not be sufficient in itself to cast doubt on the affirmations of the written witnesses.*[42] (The italics are ours.)

D. Archaeology Vs. Literary Criticism?

Our presentation of the history of archaeology may have seemed to set this branch of study against the analysis of the Scriptures by literary criticism. This should not be taken to mean that literary analysis is not a necessary and useful tool, but only that the presuppositions which have guided literary critics in the past have proven to be unrealistic and unproductive. The canons of logic and consistency employed by the critics are now shown to be theoretical ones set down by deduction rather than empirical principles learned by induction.

To cite an extreme case, Paul Haupt in a collection of essays dedicated to Wellhausen and published in 1914, reduced the Song of Deborah by thirty percent by omitting every trace of repetitive parallelism. To Haupt such repetitions were redundant and meaningless. We now know from Akkadian, Ugaritic, and other literatures that such parallelism is the very essence of Near Eastern poetry.

Noth's reconstruction of the patriarchal period and the Conquest was a masterpiece of logical erudition. Yet he failed to take into account the irrationality of human history by making the form critical method his infallible rule. As early as the 1920's Rudolph Kittel and Hugo Gressmann saw that literary criticism as it was being practiced had reached the point of steadily diminishing returns. Scholars who recognize the value of literary analysis have asked for more objective criteria by which we can assess the critic's own presuppositions. In a review of a recent commentary, Professor George Landes of Union Theological Seminary writes:

This is not to deny either the necessity or value in literary source analysis, but it does raise the question concerning the degree to which this can now be fruitfully pursued in any detailed fashion before there takes place a complete reassessment of the criteria for distinguishing the Pentateuchal literary sources in light of the implications emerging from recent studies of the way Israel's ancient Near Eastern neighbors composed and wrote their literature.[43]

Instead of functioning as an adversary of literary criticism, archaeology can and should be its ally by providing empirical data for informed criticism, much as Milman Parry's work with Slavic and Modern Greek poets has transformed Homeric criticism. Because of the abundance of unpublished materials most Near Eastern scholars have devoted themselves to the publication of new texts, so that there has been relatively little comparative work in the literary criticism of Egyptian or Babylonian literature.[44] Moshe Greenberg has written:

> It seems to me that the materials of ancient Near Eastern literature have not yet been tapped adequately by tradition and form criticism. . . . But a study of their literary styles and habits, especially with an eye to the differences between our expectations and their performance, would put solid ground under the feet of the man who would speak confidently about what may and may not be expected in a piece of ancient Near Eastern literature.[45]

The narrative style of the story of David seemed to be without close parallels in Mesopotamian and Egyptian literature, but we now have a comparable text in the inscription of Idrimi from Alalakh. [46] Albright and his disciples, by comparing the Ugaritic texts, have been able to show that many of the Psalms and poetical passages in the Old Testament are much older than modern critics have often supposed. It is this type of comparative criticism based on the fruits of archaeology which promises to be most fruitful for a better appreciation of the Bible in its cultural context.

E. A Final Word

In the light of past discoveries one may expect that future archaeological finds will continue to support the biblical traditions against radical reconstructions. Such finds will no doubt further illuminate the background of both the Old Testament and the New, making clear what has been obscure.

Those who a priori restrict the Scriptures to the human plane will find them interesting historical documents. Those who believe that God has spoken through His prophets and in His Son will find that the Bible is God's Living Word ministering to their needs today. The latter will be encouraged to know that the biblical traditions are not a patchwork of legends but are reliable records of men and women who have responded to the revelation of God in history.

To Christians, Jesus Christ is the focal point of history. They believe that the Old Testament was a prologue to His advent. The uniqueness and grandeur of Jehovah's revelation to Israel as the only true God may be better appreciated in the light which archaeology has shed on the crude, anthropomorphic polytheism of Israel's neighbors. Neither the abortive monotheism of Akhnaton's Aton nor the syncretism of Babylon's Marduk can compare with Israel's holy and compassionate Jehovah.

In like manner the life of Jesus Christ may be better assessed because of our improved knowledge of His contemporaries. But even Qumran's Teacher of Righteousness, who has been compared with Jesus and who may be His closest rival, is nowhere His peer. A comparison with the Essene Teacher but highlights the solitary splendor of the life and ministry of Jesus—the only one who could dare to claim for Himself a life of sinlessness and equality with a holy God. Others such as Roman emperors and Egyptian pharaohs may have claimed the divinity of pagan gods but their lives betray the fact that they were but mortal men.

Christians believe that Jesus' unique claim was validated by His resurrection. Archaeology may show to us the nature of Christ's tomb. But it can never be a substitute for that personal faith which carries the believer beyond the empty tomb to a living relationship with the Christ who today sits at the right hand of the Father.

Selected Bibliography

The following bibliography includes: (1) all books, and (2) those articles which have been cited more than once in the documentation accompanying the text.

_____. Albright, W. F. "Abram the Hebrew: A New Archaeological Interpretation." *Bulletin of the American Schools of Oriental Research*, no. 163 (1961), 36–54.

_____. *The Archaeology of Palestine*. Harmondsworth: Penguin Books, 1960.

_____. *Archaeology, Historical Analogy, and Early Biblical Tradition*. Baton Rouge: Louisiana State University Press, 1966.

_____. *The Biblical Period from Abraham to Ezra*. New York: Harper and Row, 1963.

_____. *From the Stone Age to Christianity*. Garden City, N.Y.: Doubleday and Co., 1957.

_____. *History, Archaeology and Christian Humanism*. New York: McGraw-Hill, 1964.

_____. *New Horizons in Biblical Research*. London: Oxford University Press, 1966.

_____. *Recent Discoveries in Bible Lands*. New York: Funk and Wagnalls, 1955.

_____. "Retrospect and Prospect in New Testament Archaeology." *The Teacher's Yoke*. Edited by E. Jerry Vardaman. Waco: Baylor University Press, 1964.

_____. *Yahweh and the Gods of Canaan*. Garden City, N.Y.: Doubleday and Co., 1968.

Aldred, Cyril. *The Egyptians*. London: Thames and Hudson, 1961.

Allegro, John. *The Dead Sea Scrolls*. Baltimore: Penguin Books, 1956.

_____. *The Treasure of the Copper Scroll*. Garden City, N.Y.: Doubleday and Co., 1964.

Archaeological Institute of America. *Archaeological Discoveries in the Holy Land*. New York: Thomas Y. Crowell, 1967.

Archer, Gleason L. *A Survey of Old Testament Introduction*. Chicago: Moody Press, 1964.

Bagatti, P. B. and Milik, J. T. *Gli Scavi del "Dominus Flevit."* Jerusalem: Studium Biblicum Franciscanum, 1958.

Barnett, R. D. *Illustrations of Old Testament History.* London: Trustees of the British Museum, 1966.

Beegle, Dewey M. *The Inspiration of Scripture.* Philadelphia: Westminster Press, 1963.

Beek, Martin A. *Atlas of Mesopotamia.* London: Nelson, 1962.

Bright, John. *Early Israel in Recent History Writing.* London: SCM Press, 1956.

Brown, Raymond E. *New Testament Essays.* Garden City, N.Y.: Doubleday and Co., 1965.

Brownlee, William H. *The Meaning of the Qumran Scrolls for the Bible.* New York: Oxford University Press, 1964.

Bruce, F. F. *The New Testament Documents.* London: Inter-Varsity Fellowship, 1960.

Burrows, Millar. *What Mean These Stones?* New York: Meridian Books, 1956.

Cadbury, H. J. *The Book of Acts in History.* London: Adam & Charles Black, 1955.

Conzelmann, Hans. *The Theology of St. Luke.* New York: Harper and Row, 1961.

Cottrell, Leonard. *The Lost Pharaohs.* New York: Grosset and Dunlap, 1961.

Cross, Frank M. *The Ancient Library of Qumran and Modern Biblical Studies.* Garden City, N.Y.: Doubleday and Co., 1961.

Cullmann, Oscar. *Peter: Disciple, Apostle, Martyr.* Philadelphia: Westminster Press, 1962.

Deiss, Joseph J. *Herculaneum: Italy's Buried Treasure.* New York: Crowell, 1970.

Deissmann, Adolf. *Light from the Ancient East.* Grand Rapids: Baker Book House, 1965 reprint of the 1922 edition.

Desroche-Noblecourt, Christiane. *Tutankhamen.* New York: Graphic Society, 1963.

Dougherty, Raymond F. *Nabonidus and Belshazzar.* New Haven: Yale University Press, 1929.

Douglas, J. D., ed. *The New Bible Dictionary.* Grand Rapids: Wm. B. Eerdmans Pub. Co., 1962.

Dupont-Sommer, A. *The Dead Sea Scrolls.* Oxford: Basil Blackwell, 1952.

_____. *The Essene Writings from Qumran.* Cleveland: World Pub. Co., 1961.

Ehrhardt, A. T. *The Framework of the New Testament Stories.* Manchester: Manchester University Press, 1964.

Finegan, Jack. *The Archeology of the New Testament.* Princeton: Princeton University Press, 1964.

_____. *Handbook of Biblical Chronology.* Princeton: Princeton University Press, 1964.

Franken, H. J., and Franken-Battershill, C. A. *A Primer of Old Testament Archaeology.* Leiden: E. J. Brill, 1963.

Freedman, David N. and Wright, G. Ernest, ed. *The Biblical Archaeologist Reader.* Garden City, N.Y.: Doubleday and Co., 1961.

———, and Greenfield, Jonas C., ed. *New Directions in Biblical Archaeology.* Garden City, N.Y.: Doubleday and Co., 1969.

Gasque, W. Ward. *Sir William Ramsay.* Grand Rapids: Baker Book House, 1966.

Glock, Albert E. "Early Israel as the Kingdom of Yahweh," in *A Symposium on Archaeology and Theology.* (see below)

Glueck, Nelson. *Rivers in the Desert.* New York: Grove Press, 1960.

Gordon, Cyrus H. *The Ancient Near East.* New York: W. W. Norton, 1965.

Gray, John. *Archaeology and the Old Testament World.* New York: Harper and Row, 1962.

Greenberg, Moshe. *The Hab/piru.* New Haven: American Oriental Soc., 1955.

Guarducci, Margherita. *The Tomb of St. Peter.* New York: Hawthorn Books, 1960.

Hahn, Herbert F. *The Old Testament in Modern Research.* Philadelphia: Fortress Press, 1966.

Hallo, William W. "From Qarqar to Carchemish: Assyria and Israel in the Light of New Discoveries." *The Biblical Archaeologist,* XXIII (May, 1960), 33–61.

Hanfmann, George. "Archaeology and the Origins of Greek Culture: Notes on Recent Work in Asia Minor." *The Antioch Review,* (spring, 1965), pp. 41–59.

Haran, Menahem, ed. *Yehezkel Kaufmann Jubilee Volume.* Jerusalem: Magnes Press, 1960.

Heidel, Alexander. *The Babylonian Genesis.* Chicago: University of Chicago Press, 1951.

———. *The Gilgamesh Epic and Old Testament Parallels.* Chicago: University of Chicago Press, 1949.

Hodgson, P. C. *The Formation of Historical Theology: A Study of F. C. Baur.* New York: Harper and Row, 1966.

Holt, John Marshall, *The Patriarchs of Israel.* Nashville: Vanderbilt University Press, 1964.

Hyatt, J. Philip, ed. *The Bible in Modern Scholarship.* Nashville: Abingdon Press, 1965.

Karrer, Otto. *Peter and the Church.* New York: Herder and Herder, 1963.

Kaufmann, Yehezkel. *The Biblical Account of the Conquest of Palestine.* Jerusalem: Magnes Press, 1953.

Kelso, James L. *et al. The Excavation of Bethel (1934–1960).* Cambridge, Mass.: American Schools of Oriental Research, 1968.

———, and Baramki, Dimitri C. *Excavations at New Testament Jericho and Khirbeten-Nitla.* New Haven: American Schools of Oriental Research, 1955.

Kenyon, Kathleen M. *Archaeology in the Holy Land.* New York: Frederick A. Praeger, 1960.

———. *Digging up Jericho.* New York: Frederick A. Praeger, 1957.

———. *Jerusalem, Excavating 3,000 Years of History.* London: Thames and Hudson, 1967.

Kitchen, K. A. *Ancient Orient and Old Testament.* Chicago: Inter-Varsity Press, 1966.

Lambert, W. G. and Millard, A. R. *Atrahasis: The Babylonian Story of the Flood.* Oxford: Clarendon Press, 1969.

Lapp, Paul W. *Biblical Archaeology and History.* New York: World Pub. Co., 1969.

———. "Palestine: Known But Mostly Unknown." *The Biblical Archaeologist,* XXVI (Dec., 1963), 121–34.

Lloyd, Seton. *Mounds of the Near East.* Edinburgh: Edinburgh University Press, 1963.

Lorimer, Hilda. *Homer and the Monuments.* London: Macmillan, 1950.

Mansoor, Menahem. *The Dead Sea Scrolls.* Grand Rapids: Wm. B. Eerdmans Pub. Co., 1964.

Mendenhall, George E. *Law and Covenant in Israel and the Ancient Near East.* Pittsburgh: Biblical Colloquium, 1955.

Montet, Pierre. *Egypt and the Bible.* Philadelphia: Fortress Press, 1968.

Myers, Jacob M. *Ezra, Nehemiah.* Garden City, N.Y.: Doubleday and Co., 1965.

———. *I Chronicles.* Garden City, N.Y.: Doubleday and Co., 1965.

———. II Chronicles. Garden City, N.Y.: Doubleday and Co., 1965.

Nineham, D. E. *et al. Historicity and Chronology in the New Testament.* London: S.P.C.K., 1965.

Noth, Martin. *The Old Testament World.* Philadelphia: Fortress Press, 1966.

O'Connor, Daniel Wm. *Peter in Rome: The Literary, Liturgical, and Archeological Evidence.* New York: Columbia University Press, 1969.

Oppenheim, A. Leo. *Ancient Mesopotamia.* Chicago: University of Chicago Press, 1964.

Page, Denys L. *History and the Homeric Iliad.* Berkeley: University of California Press, 1959.

Parrot, André. *Abraham and His Times.* Philadelphia: Fortress Press, 1968.

Selected Bibliography

———. *Discovering Buried Worlds*. London: SCM Press, 1955.

———. *Nineveh and the Old Testament*. New York: Philosophical Library, 1955.

Payne, J. B., ed. *New Perspectives on the Old Testament*. Waco: Word Books, 1970.

Pfeiffer, Robert H. *Introduction to the Old Testament*. New York: Harper and Brothers, 1941.

Picard, Gilbert. *The Ancient Civilization of Rome*. New York: Cowles Book Co., 1969.

Posener, Georges. *Leçon Inaugurale*. Paris: Collège de France, 1962.

Pritchard, James B., ed. *Ancient Near Eastern Texts Relating to the Old Testament*. Princeton: Princeton University Press, 1955.

Rainey, A. F. "Bethel Is Still *Beitîn*," *Westminster Theological Journal*, XXXIII (1971), 175–88.

Ramsay, William M. *The Bearing of Recent Discovery on the Trustworthiness of the New Testament*. London: Hodder and Stoughton, 1915.

———. *St. Paul the Traveller and the Roman Citizen*. Grand Rapids: Baker Book House, 1962 reprint of the 1897 edition.

———. *Was Christ Born at Bethlehem?* London: Hodder and Stoughton, 1898.

Ringgren, Helmer. *The Faith of Qumran*. Philadelphia: Fortress Press, 1963.

Rowley, H. H. *Darius the Mede and the Four World Empires in the Book of Daniel*. Cardiff: University of Wales Press, 1935.

Saggs, H. W. F. *Assyriology and the Study of the Old Testament*. Cardiff: University of Wales Press, 1969.

Saller, S. and Testa, E. *The Archaeological Setting of the Shrine of Bethphage*. Jerusalem: Franciscan Press, 1961.

Samuel, Alan. *The Mycenaeans in History*. Englewood Cliffs, N.J.: Prentice-Hall, 1966.

Sanders, James A., ed. *Near Eastern Archaeology in the Twentieth Century*. Garden City, N.Y.: Doubleday and Co., 1970.

Sherwin-White, A. N. *Roman Society and Roman Law in the New Testament*. Oxford: Clarendon Press, 1963.

Smith, Morton. "The Present Status of Old Testament Studies." *Journal of Biblical Literature*, LXXXVIII (1969), 19–35.

Smith, Sidney. *Babylonian Historical Texts*. London: Methuen, 1924.

Snodgrass, Anthony. *Early Greek Armour and Weapons*. Edinburgh: Edinburgh University Press, 1964.

Speiser, E. A. *Genesis*. Garden City, N.Y.: Doubleday and Co., 1964.

Stauffer, Ethelbert. *Jesus and the Wilderness Community at Qumran*. Philadelphia: Fortress Press, 1964.

The Stones and The Scriptures

Stendahl, Krister, ed. *The Scrolls and the New Testament*. New York: Harper and Brothers, 1957.

A Symposium on Archaeology and Theology. Saint Louis, Mo.: Concordia Pub. House, 1970.

Theron, Daniel J. *Evidence of Tradition*. Grand Rapids: Baker Book House, 1958.

Thomas, D. Winton, ed. *Archaeology and Old Testament Study*. London: Oxford University Press, 1967.

––––––, ed. *Documents from Old Testament Times*. New York: Harper and Brothers, 1968.

Thompson, R. J. *Moses and the Law in a Century of Criticism Since Graf*. Leiden: E. J. Brill, 1970.

Toynbee, Jocelyn and Perkins, J. Ward. *The Shrine of St. Peter and the Vatican Excavations*. London: Longmans, Green and Co., 1956.

Unger, Merrill F. *Archaeology and the New Testament*. Grand Rapids: Zondervan Pub. House, 1962.

––––––. *Archaeology and the Old Testament*. Grand Rapids: Zondervan Pub. House, 1956.

Vardaman, E. Jerry, ed. *The Teacher's Yoke*. Waco: Baylor University Press, 1964.

Vergote, J. *Joseph en Egypte*. Louvain: Publications Universitaires, 1959.

Vermueule, Emily. *Greece in the Bronze Age*. Chicago: University of Chicago Press, 1964.

Wace, A. J. B. and Stubbings, F. H., ed. *A Companion to Homer*. London: Macmillan, 1962.

Warmington, B. H. *Nero: Reality and Legend*. London: Chatto and Windus, 1969.

Wellhausen, J. *Prolegomena to the History of Israel*. Edinburgh: L. and C. Black, 1885.

Wheeler, Mortimer. *Flames over Persepolis*. New York: Reynal and Co., 1968.

Whitcomb, John C. *Darius the Mede*. Grand Rapids: Wm. B. Eerdmans Pub. Co., 1959.

Williamson, G. A. *The World of Josephus*. London: Secker and Warburg, 1964.

Wiseman, D. J. *Chronicles of Chaldaean Kings in the British Museum*. London: the Trustees of the British Museum, 1956.

––––––, et al. *Notes on Some Problems in the Book of Daniel*. London: Tyndale Press, 1965.

Woolley, C. Leonard. *A Forgotten Kingdom*. Baltimore: Penguin Books, 1953.

172

Selected Bibliography

_____. *Ur of the Chaldees.* New York: W. W. Norton, 1965 reprint of the 1929 edition.

Wright, G. Ernest, ed. *The Bible and the Ancient Near East.* Garden City, N.Y.: Doubleday and Co., 1961.

_____. *Biblical Archaeology.* Philadelphia: Westminster Press, 1962.

_____. *Schechem: the Biography of a Biblical City.* London: Gerald Duckworth and Co., 1965.

Yadin, Yigael. *The Art of Warfare in Biblical Lands.* London: Weidenfeld and Nicolson, 1963.

_____. *Masada.* New York: Random House, 1966.

_____. *The Message of the Scrolls.* New York: Grosset and Dunlap, 1962.

Yahuda, A. S. *The Language of the Pentateuch in Its Relation to Egyptian.* London: Oxford University Press, 1933.

Yamauchi, Edwin M. *Composition and Corroboration in Classical and Biblical Studies.* Philadelphia: Presbyterian and Reformed Pub. Co., 1966.

_____. *Gnostic Ethics and Mandaean Origins.* Cambridge, Mass.: Harvard University Press, 1970.

_____. *Greece and Babylon: Early Contacts between the Aegean and the Near East.* Grand Rapids: Baker Book House, 1967.

Yaron, Reuven. *The Laws of Eshnunna.* Jerusalem: Magnes Press, 1969.

Notes

Introduction

1. W. F. Albright, *The Archaeology of Palestine*, p. 219.
2. R. de Vaux, "On Right and Wrong Uses of Archaeology," in *Near Eastern Archaeology in the Twentieth Century*, ed. James A. Sanders, pp. 64–80.
3. D. J. Wiseman, "Archaeology and Scripture," *The Westminster Theological Journal*, XXXIII (1971), 151–52.
4. André Parrot, *Discovering Buried Worlds*, p. 112.
5. Millar Burrows, *What Mean These Stones?*, p. 4.
6. Dewey M. Beegle, *The Inspiration of Scripture.*
7. G. Ernest Wright, "Biblical Archaeology Today," in *New Directions in Biblical Archaeology*, ed. David N. Freedman and Jonas C. Greenfield, p. 151. Cf. Herbert F. Hahn, *The Old Testament in Modern Research*, ch. 6.
8. W. F. Albright, "Historical and Mythical Elements in the Story of Joseph," *JBL*, XXXVII (1918), 112–43.
9. W. F. Albright, "Abram the Hebrew: A New Archaeological Interpretation," *BASOR*, no. 163 (1961), 49. Cf. W. F. Albright, "Toward a More Conservative View," *Christianity Today*, VII (Jan. 8, 1963), 3–5. Reviewing his archaeological career, Albright recalls: "During these fifteen years (between World Wars) my initially rather skeptical attitude toward the accuracy of Israelite historical tradition had suffered repeated jolts as discovery after discovery confirmed the historicity of details which might reasonably have been considered legendary." W. F. Albright, *History, Archaeology and Christian Humanism*, p. 309.
10. Morton Smith, "The Present State of Old Testament Studies," *JBL*, LVIII (1969), 19–35.
11. G. Ernest Wright, "Old Testament Scholarship in Prospect," *JBR*, XXVIII (1960), 192.

Chapter One: Mari, Nuzi, and Alalakh

1. For parallel and divergent trends in classical and biblical studies see Edwin M. Yamauchi, *Composition and Corroboration in Classical and Biblical Studies*. Cf. R. J. Thompson, *Moses and the Law in a Century of Criticism Since Graf.*
2. J. Wellhausen, *Prolegomena to the History of Israel*, pp. 318 ff.

3. Cf. Denys L. Page, *History and the Homeric Iliad.*

4. John Bright, *Early Israel in Recent History Writing,* p. 84.

5. John Bright, "Modern Study of Old Testament Literature," in *The Bible and the Ancient Near East,* ed. G. Ernest Wright, p. 15.

6. W. F. Albright, *Archaeology, Historical Analogy, and Early Biblical Tradition,* p. 18. Cf. Albert E. Glock, "Early Israel as the Kingdom of Yahweh," in *A Symposium on Archaeology and Theology,* pp. 46–52.

7. Albright, *History, Archaeology,* pp. 265–66. The First World War interrupted the work of the Deutsches Evangelisches Institut in Palestine. Its topographical seminars were resumed in 1924. After the Second World War, the Institute's activities were begun again in 1953. With the exception of a small dig at Madeba in recent years, the Germans have not conducted any excavations in the Holy Land since World War I.

8. For an examination of this outlook, see Walter C. Kaiser, "The Literary Form of Genesis 1–11," in *New Perspectives on the Old Testament,* ed. J. B. Payne, pp. 48–65.

9. W. G. Lambert, "A New Look at the Babylonian Background of Genesis," *Journal of Theological Studies,* XVI (1965), 287–300.

10. Leonard Woolley, *Ur of the Chaldees,* p. 29.

11. M. Mallowan, "Noah's Flood Reconsidered," *Iraq,* XXVI (1964), 62–82. R. Raikes, "The Physical Evidence for Noah's Flood," *Iraq,* XXVIII (1966), 52–63, suggests that further soundings are necessary to settle the question.

12. W. F. Albright, *Yahweh and the Gods of Canaan,* pp. 98–99; cf. G. Ernest Wright, *Biblical Archaeology,* p. 33.

13. A. R. Millard, "A New Babylonian 'Genesis' Story," *Tyndale Bulletin,* XVIII (1967), 18. Cf. W. G. Lambert and A. R. Millard, *Atraḫasīs: The Babylonian Story of the Flood.*

14. Alexander Heidel, *The Gilgamesh Epic and Old Testament Parallels,* p. 87. The daily cult in pagan temples was essentially the provision of food for the gods. In the Hittite Kumarbi Myth the god Ea warns Kumarbi that if he should destroy mankind, no one would remain to feed the gods with offerings. In the Babylonian *Pessimistic Dialogue* a servant suggests to his master that he should be able to coerce the gods by refusing to offer sacrifices. Cf. Edwin M. Yamauchi, "Anthropomorphism in Ancient Religions," *Bibliotheca Sacra,* CXXV (1968), 29–44.

15. H. H. Rowley, "Recent Discovery and the Patriarchal Age," *BJRL,* XXXII (1949–50), 79.

16. J. C. L. Gibson, "Light from Mari on the Patriarchs," *Journal of Semitic Studies,* VII (1962), 58.

17. Rowley, "The Patriarchal Age," p. 70.

18. Frank M. Cross, "The Tabernacle," *BA*, X (1947), 53.

19. D. J. Wiseman, "Alalakh," in *Archaeology and Old Testament Study* [hereafter abbreviated *AOTS*], edited by D. Winton Thomas, p. 127.

20. Nelson Glueck, *Rivers in the Deseri*, p. 74.

21. E. A. Speiser, *Genesis*, p. 107.

22. *Ibid.*, p. 108; cf. Albright, "Abram the Hebrew," pp. 49–50.

23. Martin Noth, *The Old Testament World*, p. 17.

24. *Ibid.*, p. 7.

25. W. F. Albright, *From the Stone Age to Christianity*, p. 382.

26. Albright, "Abram the Hebrew," p. 38, fn. 9; and Albright, *Archaeology, Historical Analogy*, p. 36.

27. O. Eissfeldt, *Palestine in the Time of the Nineteenth Dynasty*, p. 6.

28. Speiser, *Genesis*, p. 90. R. de Vaux, "Les Patriarches Hébreux et l'histoire," *Revue Biblique*, LXXII (1965), 16, holds that the mention of camels is not necessarily anachronistic.

29. André Parrot, *Abraham and His Times*, pp. 100–101. Pierre Montet, *Egypt and the Bible*, p. 6, cites a stone vessel in the form of a camel found at Abusir el-Melek in Egypt dating from the third millennium. Cyrus H. Gordon, *The Ancient Near East*, p. 124, notes evidence of early camel riding on seal cylinders.

30. K. A. Kitchen, *Ancient Orient and Old Testament*, p. 79.

31. Manfred R. Lehmann, "Abraham's Purchase of Machpelah and Hittite Law," *BASOR*, no. 129 (1953), 15–18. Gene M. Tucker, "The Legal Background of Genesis 23," *JBL*, has called attention to parallels with Neo-Babylonian sale documents, but this does not mean—as he argues—that the patriarchal narratives are therefore late. When both early and late parallels exist, neither can be used as the sole evidence for dating the stories.

32. H. A. Hoffner, "Some Contributions of Hittitology to Old Testament Study," *Tyndale Bulletin*, XX (1969), 27–55.

33. A. Dupont-Sommer, "Sur le débuts de l'histoire araméenne," *Supplements to Vetus Testamentum*, (1953), pp. 40–49.

34. Parrot in *AOTS*, p. 143; cf. his *Abraham and His Times*, pp. 54–55.

35. John Marshall Holt, *The Patriarchs of Israel*, p. 82.

36. E. G. Gordon, *The Ancient Near East*, p. 121.

37. For early contacts with the Aegean see Edwin M. Yamauchi, *Greece and Babylon: Early Contacts Between the Aegean and the Near East.*

38. A. S. Yahuda, *The Language of the Pentateuch in Its Relation to Egyptian*, has overstated the case but the evidence is still considerable as may be

seen in an article by O. Lambdin, "Egyptian Loan Words in the Old Testament," *JAOS*, LXXIII (1953), 145–55.

39. Theophile Meek, "Moses and the Levites," *American Journal of Semitic Languages*, LVI (1939), 113–20.

40. Scholars who accept a fifteenth century date for the Exodus would put Joseph in the nineteenth century. Most scholars would put Joseph in Egypt in the Hyksos period in the seventeenth century.

41. See Jozef Janssen, "Egyptological Remarks on *The Story of Joseph in Genesis*," *Jaarbericht Ex Oriente Lux*, 14 (1955–56), 63–72; J. Vergote, *Joseph en Égypte*; K. A. Kitchen, "Egypt and the Bible: Some Recent Advances," *Faith and Thought*, XCI (1959–60), 177–97.

42. Speiser, pp. 316–17.

43. W. F. Albright, *The Biblical Period from Abraham to Ezra*, p. 10.

44. Vergote, pp. 147–48.

45. For a recent defense of the early date of the Exodus, see Leon T. Wood, "Date of the Exodus," in Payne, *New Perspectives on the Old Testament*, pp. 66–87; in the same volume, cf. Carl E. DeVries, "The Bearing of Current Egyptian Studies on the Old Testament," pp. 25–36.

46. See the important review of Glueck's *Explorations in Eastern Palestine* by H. J. Franken and W. J. A. Power in *Vetus Testamentum*, XXI (1971), 119–23.

47. Kitchen, pp. 72–75; cf. *The New Bible Dictionary*, ed. J. D. Douglas, pp. 214–16.

48. George E. Mendenhall, *Law and Covenant in Israel and the Ancient Near East*.

49. Wright, "Old Testament Scholarship in Prospect," p. 189.

50. Albert E. Glock, Mendenhall's student, has demonstrated the antiquity of the prose narratives in Numbers describing the murmuring of the Israelites against the covenant. An examination of the sociological and military background of the narratives in comparison with Near Eastern traditions establishes "not only the antiquity of Israelite traditions but also her unique character as a dissenting and disinherited community of *hophshi* (emancipated slaves) and *habirú* (social outcasts). This is the kind of evidence that supports the general assumption that one may safely use the prose sources reflecting Israel between Moses and Samuel to reconstruct the religion of Early Israel." Glock, "Early Israel as the Kingdom of Yahweh," p. 65. Cf. also pp. 61, 89. Critics have heretofore assigned most of the narratives in Numbers 1–10 to the late Priestly source.

51. Reuven Yaron, *The Laws of Eshnunna*, p. 49. A. van Selms, "The Goring Ox in Babylonian and Biblical Law," *Archiv Orientalni*, XVIII

(1950), 321–30, points out some differences in the two traditions but the similarities are still striking.

52. Moshe Greenberg, "Some Postulates of Biblical Criminal Law," in *The Yehezkel Kaufmann Jubilee Volume*, ed. Menahem Haran, pp. 5–28.

53. Wright, *Biblical Archaeology*, p. 179, fn. 7. The exception is a metal figure of a Canaanite god found in 1958 in the Israelite level at Hazor in 1958. This was, however, in a metal hoard which may have been saved for non-ritual purposes.

54. For a recent work using this argument, see Gleason L. Archer, *A Survey of Old Testament Introduction*, pp. 254–59.

55. Moshe Greenberg, *The Hab/piru*, p. 92.

56. For a criticism of this view, see G. Ernest Wright, "The Literary and Historical Problem of Joshua 10 and Judges 1," *JNES*, V (1946), 105–14.

57. Yehezkel Kaufmann, *The Biblical Account of the Conquest of Palestine*.

58. Limited soundings by Y. Aharoni in the area of the Sun Temple at Lachish in 1968 uncovered an Israelite level, which can be dated only to *c.* 1000 B.C.

59. Moshe Dothan, "Ashdod: A City of the Philistine Pentapolis," in *Archaeological Discoveries in the Holy Land*, edited by the Archaeological Institute of America, pp. 132–33.

60. Some scholars have interpreted Josh. 11:13, "But as for the cities that stood on their mounds (lit. *tells*), Israel burned none of them, save Hazor only, that did Joshua burn," to mean that only at Hazor were any of the cities burned. Signs of burning at other Canaanite sites would then have no bearing on the Israelite Conquest or on the date of the Exodus. However, the context of verses 12 and 14 seems to indicate that this remark should be interpreted to refer only to the allies of Jabin mentioned in verse 1.

61. James L. Kelso, *The Excavation of Bethel*, p. 32. It should be noted, however, that the conquest of Bethel is not mentioned in Joshua; in Judges its conquest is described as the result of treason.

62. *Ibid.*, p. 49.

63. James F. Ross in *Archaeological Discoveries in the Holy Land*, p. 124. Cf. Edward F. Campbell and James F. Ross, "The Excavation of Shechem and the Biblical Tradition," *BA*, XXVI (1963), 10.

64. Kelso comments: "A few tomb findings now prove that Jericho was inhabited at the close of LB, confirming Pére Vincent's statement about the presence of such pottery on the site at the time of the German excavations." Kelso, p. 48.

65. Kathleen M. Kenyon, *Digging up Jericho*, pp. 261–62.

66. *Ibid.*, p. 262.

67. Paul W. Lapp, "Palestine: Known But Mostly Unknown," *BA*, XXVI

(Dec., 1963), 124–25. C. Umhau Wolf, "The Location of Gilgal," *Biblical Research*, XI (1966), 42–51, makes the radical suggestion that Tell es-Sultan is not Jericho but Gilgal, and that we should look for Jericho elsewhere.

68. James B. Pritchard, "Culture and History" in *The Bible in Modern Scholarship*, ed. J. Philip Hyatt, p. 319.

69. Pritchard in *Archaeological Discoveries in the Holy Land*, p. 146.

70. Anson F. Rainey, "Bethel is Still *Beitın*," *Westminster Theological Journal*, XXXIII (1971), 178.

71. Kathleen M. Kenyon, *Palestine in the Time of the Eighteenth Dynasty*, p. 23.

72. Joseph A. Callaway, "New Evidence on the Conquest of ʿAi," *JBL*, LXXXVII (1968), 312–20.

73. Callaway does not mention, however, the possibility—at least admitted by Pritchard—that the Late Bronze remains may still be uncovered at Gibeon, nor Aharoni's view that Late Bronze Arad was relocated at Tell Milh. The area supervisors of the Iron Age village at et-Tell offer a different conclusion: "Nothing in the present evidence warrants an identification of the village with the city of ʿAi captured by Joshua as described in Joshua 8:1–29." W. J. A. Power and Robert J. Bull, *BASOR*, no. 178 (1965), 27–28.

74. See the map of the 1964–69 excavations in Joseph A. Callaway, "The 1968–1969 ʿAi (et-Tell) Excavations," *BASOR*, no. 198 (1970), 9. It may be noted in passing that in 1928 John Garstang found outside the et-Tell city wall a single wish-bone handle of (Late Bronze) Cypriote ware.

75. David Livingston, "Location of Biblical Bethel and Ai Reconsidered," *Westminster Theological Journal*, XXXIII (1970), 20–44, has attempted to resolve the problem by arguing that Ai cannot be at et-Tell as Bethel is not to be located at Beitin, the former identification being dependent upon the latter. This radical proposal is countered by Rainey's article, cited in note 70 above.

76. Paul W. Lapp, *Biblical Archaeology and History*, p. 109.

77. *Ibid.*, p. 110. Cf. Paul W. Lapp, "The Conquest of Palestine in the Light of Archaeology," *Concordia Theological Monthly*, XXXVIII (1967), 283–300.

78. H. Keith Beebe, "Ancient Palestinian Dwellings," *BA*, XXXI (May, 1968), 49.

79. Albright, *The Biblical Period*, pp. 30–31.

80. Kelso, p. 34.

81. Wright, *Biblical Archaeology*, p. 70.

82. G. Ernest Wright in *AOTS*, pp. 364–65. Cf. G. Ernest Wright, *Shechem*, pp. 100–102.

83. The name of the Philistine ruler or *seren* may be related to the Greek *tyrannos* "tyrant," which seems to be a Lydian loan word. The Philistine headdress appears on the Phaistos Disk from Crete, and Philistine pottery is based on Mycenaean IIIC prototypes. Recent excavations at Ashdod have revealed striking parallels with Greek figurines of the Mycenaean period, and have uncovered seals with Cypro-Minoan scripts.

84. Cf. Frank Stubbings, "Arms and Armour," *A Companion to Homer*, ed. Alan Wace and Frank Stubbings, p. 505.

85. Wiseman in *AOTS*, p. 128.

86. W. F. Albright, "The Impact of Archaeology on Biblical Research—1966," in Freedman, *New Directions*, p. 10.

87. Morton Smith, "The Present State of Old Testament Studies," *JBL*, LXXXVIII (1969), 30–31.

88. Albright, *History, Archaeology*, p. 35.

89. M. E. L. Mallowan in *AOTS*, p. 62.

90. Yigael Yadin, *The Art of Warfare in Biblical Lands*, p. 288.

91. In March, 1969, Beno Rothenberg discovered at the base of the so-called "Solomon's Pillars," a favorite tourist site at Timna just north of Elath, an Egyptian temple with inscriptions of the XIX–XXth Dynasties from Seti I (1318–1304) down to Ramesses V (1160–1156). Rothenberg now suggests that it was these Egyptian kings of the fourteenth–twelfth centuries rather than the Judean kings of the tenth–sixth centuries who were responsible for the copper mines in the Arabah. Beno Rothenberg, "King Solomon's Mines No More," *Illustrated London News*, (Nov. 15, 1969), 32–33; "The Egyptian Temple of Timna," *Illustrated London News*, (Nov. 29, 1969); cf. "Notes and News," *PEQ*, CI (1969) 57–59. This revision has now been accepted by W. F. Albright, *BASOR*, no. 202 (1971), 4.

92. Nelson Glueck, "Ezion-geber," *BA*, XXVIII (1965), 73; and "Further Explorations in the Negev," *BASOR*, no. 179 (1965), 17.

93. Glueck, *Rivers in the Desert*, p. 31.

94. R. D. Barnett, *Illustrations of Old Testament History*, p. 40. Jonas Greenfield, however, believes that *'lmg/'lgm* was not sandalwood but a tree that grew in Lebanon. *JAOS*, LXXXIX (1969), 138.

95. W. F. Albright, "The Role of the Canaanites in the History of Civilization," in Wright, *The Bible and the Ancient Near East*, p. 348.

96. A South Arabian stamp from *c.* 9th century, found at Bethel, has been claimed as evidence confirming Solomon's contacts with the queen of Sheba in Arabia. G. W. van Beek, and A. Jamme, "An Inscribed South Arabian Clay Stamp from Bethel." *BASOR*, no. 151 (1958), 15–16; cf. *BASOR*, no. 163 (1961), 15–18. However, after an examina-

tion of photographic evidence Yadin argues that the Bethel seal is none other than a seal acquired by an Englishman at the turn of the century, which has mysteriously found its way to Palestine from England. Yigael Yadin, "An Inscribed South-Arabian Clay Stamp from Bethel?" *BASOR*, no. 196 (1969), 37–45. On the other hand, G. W. Van Beek and A. Jamme, "The Authenticity of the Bethel Stamp Seal," *BASOR*, no. 199 (1970), 59–65, and James L. Kelso, "A Reply to Yadin's Article on the Finding of the Bethel Seal," *ibid.*, p. 65, have sought to refute Yadin's arguments and have reaffirmed the authors' conviction in the authenticity of the seal.

97. H. J. Franken and C. A. Franken-Battershill. *A Primer of Old Testament Archaeology*, p. 99.

98. *DOTT*, p. 196.

99. Wright, *Biblical Archaeology*, p. 158.

100. *DOTT*, p. 48.

101. *Ibid.*, pp. 242–50.

102. *Ibid.*, p. 55.

103. André Parrot, *Nineveh and the Old Testament*, pp. 44–45.

104. William W.. Hallo, "From Qarqar to Carchemish: Assyria and Israel in the Light of New Discoveries," *BA*, XXIII (May, 1960), 51.

105. *DOTT*, p. 60.

106. Hallo, p. 56.

107. *DOTT*, p. 210.

108. The text was first published in *Iraq*, XVII (1955), plate IV, lines 13–24. The translation is taken from H. W. F. Saggs, *Assyriology and the Study of the Old Testament*, p. 17.

109. *Ibid.*, p. 18.

110. Kitchen, pp. 82–83.

111. *DOTT*, p. 67.

112. Scholars are divided as to the date of the destruction of Level III on the summit of Lachish. Tufnell and Barnett date this to the Assyrian attack of 701; Starkey, Wright, Kenyon, and Albright favor a later attack by Nebuchadnezzar in 597.

113. R. D. Barnett, "The Siege of Lachish," *IEJ*, VIII (1958), 161–64.

114. J. A. Brinkman, "Elamite Military Aid to Merodach-Baladan," *JNES*, XXIV (1965), 161–66.

115. Jerome D. Quinn, "Alcaeus 48 (B16) and the Fall of Ascalon (604 B.C.)." *BASOR*, no. 164 (1961), 19–20.

116. John Bright, "A New Letter in Aramaic, Written to a Pharaoh of Egypt," in *The Biblical Archaeologist Reader*, ed. David N. Freedman and G. Ernest Wright, p. 105.

117. In 1967 Aharoni's excavation at Arad west of the Dead Sea brought to light a Hebrew ostracon which tells a dramatic tale. The ostracon urgently orders soldiers to Ramath-negeb (perhaps Khirbet Ghazzeh) in view of an imminent Edomite attack (cf. Ezek. 35:15). Aharoni suggests that this attack came about 600 B.C. just before Nebuchadnezzar destroyed Arad. Y. Aharoni, "Three Hebrew Ostraca from Arad," *BASOR*, no. 197 (1970), 16–42.

118. *DOTT*, p. 79.

119. *Ibid.*, p. 80.

120. *Ibid.*, p. 216. In 1963 Joseph Naveh published a group of graffiti which had been scratched on the wall of a tomb at Khirbet Beit Lei five miles east of Lachish. He translates the longest inscription as follows: "Yahveh (is) the God of the whole earth; the mountains of Judah [Yĕhūd!] belong to him, to the God of Jerusalem." J. Naveh, "Old Hebrew Inscriptions in a Burial Cave," *IEJ*, XIII (1963), 74–96. Frank M. Cross, "The Cave Inscriptions from Khirbet Beit Lei," in Sanders, *Near Eastern Archaeology*, pp. 299–306, translates this inscription as follows: "I am Yahweh thy God: I will accept the cities of Judah, and will redeem Jerusalem." Cross believes that the graffiti may have been incised by a refugee fleeing from the destruction of Jerusalem in 587. They would then represent an affirmation of faith in God's faithfulness in spite of the desolation of the Holy City. Cf. Lam. 3:22–24.

121. Kathleen M. Kenyon, *Archaeology in the Holy Land*, p. 291.

122. Albright, *History, Archaeology*, p. 32.

123. Saul S. Weinberg, "Post-Exilic Palestine: An Archaeological Report," *Proceedings of the Israel Academy of Sciences and Humanities*, IV, no. 5 (1969), 84. He suggests that the evidence for a truer picture of the post-Exilic period may be furnished to us by a study of the many nameless sites with sixth–fifth century pottery which the recent Israeli surveys of Judah have discovered. I am indebted to Professor Weinberg for supplying me with an advance copy of his article.

124. W. F. Albright, "King Joiachin in Exile," *BA*, V (Dec., 1942), 49–55.

125. *DOTT*, p. 93.

126. David N. Freedman in Hyatt, p. 307.

127. E. J. Bickerman, "The Edict of Cyrus in Ezra 1," *JBL*, LXV (1946), 249–75.

128. Isaac Rabinowitz, "Aramaic Inscriptions of the Fifth Century BCE from a North-Arab Shrine in Egypt," *JNES*, XV (1956), 1–9.

129. W. F. Albright, *Recent Discoveries in Bible Lands*, p. 105, observes: "The trend of recent study has been strongly in favor of raising the date of the compilation of the Chronicler's work from the third century (as supposed by nearly all competent scholars of the past generation) to the early fourth. With this goes a correspondingly higher respect for its

historical value." Cf. the recent commentaries on Chronicles and Ezra-Nehemiah by Jacob Myers in the Anchor Bible Series, in which the date of 400 B.C. is suggested for these works.

130. J. Weingreen in *DOTT*, p. 232.

131. H. H. Rowley, *Darius the Mede and the Four World Empires in the Book of Daniel*, p. 57.

132. John Whitcomb, *Darius the Mede*.

133. D. J. Wiseman *et al.*, *Notes on Some Problems in the Book of Daniel*, pp. 9–18.

134. Raymond F. Dougherty, *Nabonidus and Belshazzar*, p. 200.

135. A. Leo Oppenheim's translation of the "Verse Account of Nabonidus, " in *Ancient Near Eastern Texts Relating to the Old Testament*, ed. James B. Pritchard, p. 313.

136. For the new Haran texts see C. J. Gadd, "The Harran Inscriptions of Nabonidus," *Anatolian Studies*, VIII (1958), 35–92.

137. A. K. Grayson and W. G. Lambert, "Akkadian Prophecies," *Journal of Cuneiform Studies*, XVIII (1964), 10.

138. J. Nevah, "The Excavations at Mesad-Hashavyahu—Preliminary Report," *IEJ*, XII (1962), 89–113.

139. Y. Aharoni, "Hebrew Ostraca from Tel Arad," *IEJ*, XVI (1966), 4.

140. W. F. Albright, "Cilicia and Babylonia under the Chaldean Kings," *BASOR*, no. 120 (1950), 25.

141. For other evidences of Greek influence in the Near East before Alexander see Yamauchi, *Greece and Babylon*, and "The Greek Words in Daniel in the Light of Greek Influence in the Near East," in Payne, *New Perspectives on the Old Testament*, pp. 170–200.

142. On the question of the Hebrew and the Aramaic of Daniel, see the articles by W. J. Martin and K. A. Kitchen in Wiseman, *Some Problems in Daniel*.

143. The recent discovery of manuscripts of Daniel at Qumran, some as early as 120 B.C., does not conclusively prove the arguments for a late date wrong but it should raise the suspicion that the composition of Daniel must be placed earlier than the second century B.C. Cf. Jacob M. Myers, *I Chronicles*, p. LXXXVII, fn., "The presence of Chronicles, Ezra, and Nehemiah fragments among the Qumran cave IV materials makes a third century date (for the works of the Chronicler) difficult to maintain."

Chapter Two: Ramsay vs. The Tübingen School

1. P. C. Hodgson, *The Formation of Historical Theology: A Study of F. C. Baur*, argues that Baur wrote his initial formulation in 1831 before he knew of Hegel's work. But Hegel's ideas were widespread in Germany

long before this, and it seems more than coicidental that Baur's theory corresponds so closely to Hegel's thesis.

2. Johannes Munck in Hyatt, pp. 168–69.

3. *Ibid.*, pp. 172–73.

4. For an evaluation of the date of the Mandaean materials see Edwin M. Yamauchi, *Gnostic Ethics and Mandaean Origins.*

5. An important example of this recent trend is the work of Hans Conzelmann, *The Theology of St. Luke.* The work's original title in German, *Die Mitte der Zeit* "The Middle-point of Time," indicates that Luke was a creative theologian looking backward to the time of Christ and forward to the future of the Church. Conzelmann is not particularly interested in questions of historicity.

6. W. F. Albright, "Retrospect and Prospect in New Testament Archaeology," in *The Teacher's Yoke*, ed. E. Jerry Vardaman, p. 29.

7. William M. Ramsay, *St. Paul the Traveller and the Roman Citizen*, p. 8. For an account or Ramsay's life and contributions see W. Ward Gasque, *Sir William Ramsay.*

8. A. T. Olmstead, "History, Ancient World, and the Bible: Problems of Attitude and of Method," *JNES*, II (1943), 23.

9. W. W. Gasque, "The Historical Value of the Book of Acts," *Evangelical Quarterly*, XLI (1969), 83–84.

10. A. T. Ehrhardt, *The Framework of the New Testament Stories*, p. 64.

11. G. A. Williamson, *The World of Josephus*, p. 290.

12. B. H. Warmington, *Nero: Reality and Legend*, p. 9.

13. A. N. Sherwin-White, *Roman Law in the New Testament*, p. 189.

14. Lily Ross Taylor, "Quirinius and the Census of Judaea," *American Journal of Philology*, LIV (1933), 133.

15. Adolf Deissmann, *Light from the Ancient East*, p. 270.

16. Daniel J. Theron, *Evidence of Tradition*, pp. 21–22. For Ramsay's arguments, see his *Was Christ Born at Bethlehem?*

17. Jack Finegan, *Handbook of Biblical Chronology*, p. 238.

18. V. Corbo, "St. Peter's House in Capernaum Rediscovered," *Christian News from Israel*, XX, 1–2 (1969), 39–50; V. Corbo and S. Loffreda, *Ricordi di S. Pietro sul Lago di Tiberiade.*

19. In the spring of 1968 the writer had the privilege of witnessing modern Samaritans slaying the Passover lambs on top of Mount Gerizim.

20. James L. Kelso and Dimitri C. Baramki, *Excavations at New Testament Jericho and Khirbet en-Nitla*, p. 10.

21. V. Tzaferis, "Jewish Tombs at and near Giv 'at ha-Mivtar," *IEJ*, XX (1970), 18–32.

22. N. Haas, "Anthropological Observations on the Skeletal Remains from Giv at ha-Mivtar," *IEJ*, XX (1970), 58.

23. R. A. S. Macalister, "The 'Garden Tomb,'" *QS*, (1907), 231.

24. L. E. Cox Evans, "The Holy Sepulchre," *PEQ*, C (1968), 119. Early in 1971 Greek Orthodox authorities announced that remains of the Constantinian basilica, including part of an apse and the base of a column, had been found a few feet under the present pavement and about thirty feet from the traditional "Calvary."

25. Kathleen M. Kenyon, *Jerusalem, Excavating 3,000 Years of History*, p. 154.

26. Kenneth J. Conant, "The Holy Sites at Jerusalem in the First and Fourth Centuries," *Proceedings of the American Philosophical Society*, CII (1958), 16.

27. S. Saller and E. Testa, *The Archaeological Setting of the Shrine of Bethphage*, p. 73.

28. Deissmann, p. 440.

29. Cf. R. North, "The Damascus of Qumran Geography," *PEQ*, 87 (1955), 34–48.

30. For arguments in favor of the Sukenik wall as Agrippa's "third" wall see: E. W. Hamrick, "New Excavations at Sukenik's 'Third Wall,'" *BASOR*, no. 183 (1966), 19–26; and "Further Notes on the 'Third Wall,'" *BASOR*, no. 192 (1968), 21–25; M. Avi-Yonah, "The Third and Second Walls of Jerusalem," *IEJ*, XVIII (1968), 98–125.

31. For arguments in favor of the present north wall as Agrippa's "third" wall see: Kenyon, *Jerusalem*, pp. 166–68; J. B. Hennessy, "Preliminary Report on Excavations at the Damascus Gate Jerusalem, 1964–6," *Levant*, II (1970), 22–27.

32. Avi-Yonah, p. 121.

33. William M. Ramsay, *The Bearing of Recent Discovery on the Trustworthiness of the New Testament*, pp. 39–52.

34. A recently discovered inscription sheds further light on the intense devotion given to Artemis of Ephesus. Forty-five inhabitants of Sardis who are accused of maltreating a sacred embassy from Ephesus, bearing cloaks for Artemis, are condemned to die. See F. Sokolowski, "A New Testimony on the Cult of Artemis of Ephesus," *Harvard Theological Review*, LVIII (1965), 427–31.

35. Alfons Wotschitzky, "Ephesus: Past, Present, and Future of a Great Metropolis," *Archaeology*, XIV (1961), 209.

36. H. J. Cadbury, *The Book of Acts in History*, p. 41.

37. Deissmann, p. 80.

38. *Ibid.*, p. 354.

39. A. N. Sherwin-White, "The Trial of Christ," in D. E. Nineham *et al.*, *Historicity and Chronology in the New Testament*, p. 101.

40. E. L. Sukenik, "The Earliest Records of Christianity," *AJA*, LI (1947), 351–65.

41. P. B. Bagatti and J. T. Milik, *Gli Scavi del "Dominus Flevit,"* p. 179, would restore the first inscription to read *IOUDA*, that is, Jesus the son of Judah. But Sukenik declared flatly that there were no letters after the IOU. Erich Dinkler, "Zur Geschichte des Kreuzsymbols," *Zeitschrift für Theologie und Kirche*, XLVIII (1951), 155–56, would take both *IOU* and *ALŌTH* as personal names, citing parallels from Egyptian papyri. The first he takes as a genitive of the name *IAS*, found in a fourth century A.D. papyrus; *ALŌTH* is found in a second century A.D. papyrus.

42. B. Gustafson, "The Oldest Graffiti in the History of the Church," *NTS*, III (1956–57), 64–69. On the other hand, D. Fishwick, "The Talpioth Ossuaries Again," *NTS*, X (1963), 49–61, interprets the inscriptions as magical incantations using the name Jesus. However, the Greek magical papyri from Egypt that Fishwick uses for his parallels date mainly from the fourth century A.D., and there are no comparable magical parallels from the ossuary inscriptions.

43. Finegan, *The Archaeology of the New Testament*, p. 242.

44. *Ibid.*, pp. 243–49.

45. *Ibid.*, pp. 220 ff., contains a detailed discussion of the history of the cross mark.

46. J. Jothams-Rothschild, "The Tombs of Sanhedria," *PEQ*, LXXXVI (1954), 19–20.

47. Finegan, pp. 249–50. Cf. Joseph Deiss, *Herculaneum: Italy's Buried Treasure*, pp. 36, 65, 68 f., 79.

48. Floyd Filson, "Were There Christians in Pompeii? *BA*, II (May, 1939), 13–16.

49. D. Fishwick, "On the Origin of the ROTAS-SATOR Square," *Harvard Theological Review*, LVII (1964), 39–53, argues that the anagram was a magical square worked out by the Jews of Pompeii, which was later adopted by the Christians.

50. Cf. Jocelyn Toynbee and J. Ward Perkins, *The Shrine of St. Peter and the Vatican Excavations.*

51. Margherita Guarducci, *The Tomb of St. Peter.*

52. Graydon F. Snyder, "Survey and 'New' Thesis on the Bones of Peter," *BA*, XXXII (Feb., 1969), 11–14.

53. Oscar Cullmann, *Peter: Disciple, Apostle, Martyr*, p. 156. For a Roman Catholic response to Cullmann's appraisal, see Otto Karrer, *Peter and*

the Church. Daniel Wm. O'Connor, *Peter in Rome: The Literary, Liturgical, and Archeological Evidence,* p. 209, concludes that it appears *more plausible than not* that Peter's death in the Vatican area was remembered "in the traditions of the Church and in the erection of a simple monument near the place where he died." O'Connor suggests that: "His body was never recovered for burial by the Christian group which later, when relics became of great importance for apologetic reasons, came to believe that what originally had marked the general area of his death also indicated the precise placement of his grave."

Chapter Three: Qumran and the Essenes

1. Yigael Yadin, *The Message of the Scrolls,* p. 19–20.

2. *Ibid.,* p. 41.

3. Frank M. Cross, "The Early History of the Qumran Community," in Freedman, *New Directions,* pp. 66–67.

4. In addition to the Nash Papyrus, there were some quotations in the Aramaic magic bowls of the sixth century A.D. from Iraq and Iran. See Edwin M. Yamauchi, "Aramaic Magic Bowls," *JAOS,* LXXXV (1965), 511–23.

5. Cf. Patrick W. Skehan, "The Scrolls and the Old Testament Text," in Freedman, *New Directions,* p. 94.

6. Bruce K. Waltke, "The Samaritan Pentateuch and the Text of the Old Testament," in Payne, *New Perspectives,* pp. 212–39.

7. Yigael Yadin, "The Temple Scroll," in Freedman, *New Directions,* pp. 139–48. Cf. the same report in *BA,* XXX (Dec., 1967), 135–39. The *Los Angeles Times* (Aug. 28, 1969) reports that Israel paid an Arab dealer $150,000 for the scroll.

8. Cross, however, believes that these immersions took place either at the Ain Feshka spring two miles south or at the Jordan River at an even greater distance north. The writer believes that this is not required by the texts and would be unnecessarily inconvenient.

9. Kenneth W. Clark, "The Posture of the Ancient Scribe," *BA,* XXVI (May, 1963), 63–72.

10. In March, 1969, a small settlement nine miles south of Qumran was uncovered. The remains of a building, coins, and tombs found there resemble those of Qumran. Of the twenty tombs cleared, twelve were of men, seven of women, and one of a boy of about seven.

11. F. F. Bruce, "The Dead Sea Scrolls and Early Christianity," *BJRL,* XLIX (1966), 82.

12. Cf. Edwin M. Yamauchi, "The Present Status of Mandaean Studies," *JNES,* XXV (1966), 10–15.

13. Raymond E. Brown, *New Testament Essays*, pp. 188–89. Cf. also A. M. Hunter, "New Testament Survey 1939–1964," *Expository Times*, LXXVI (1964), 17.

14. W. F. Albright, *New Horizons in Biblical Research*, p. 49.

15. Raymond E. Brown, "The Semitic Background of the New Testament Mysterion," *Catholic Biblical Quarterly*, XX (1958), 417–43; *Biblica*, XXXIX (1958), 426–48; XL (1959), 70–87.

16. M. de Jonge and A. S. van der Woude, "11Q Melchizedek and the New Testament," *NTS*, XII (1965–66), 322.

17. Albright, "Retrospect and Prospect in New Testament Archaeology," in Vardaman, *The Teacher's Yoke*, p. 41.

18. Floyd V. Filson, "The Dead Sea Scrolls and the New Testament," in Freedman, *New Directions*, pp. 133–34.

19. The following section represents the adaptation of an article, "The Teacher of Righteousness from Qumran and Jesus of Nazareth," which appeared in *Christianity Today*, X (May 13, 1966), 12–14.

20. A. Dupont-Sommer, *The Dead Sea Scrolls*, p. 99.

21. Patrick W. Skehan, "Capriccio Allegro or How Not to Learn in Ten Years," *Christian Century*, (Oct. 5, 1966), pp. 1211–13.

22. John M. Allegro, "The Untold Story of the Dead Sea Scrolls," *Harper's Magazine*, CCXXXIII (Aug., 1966).

23. See the scathing review by a leading Aramaic scholar, Joseph A. Fitzmyer, "A Sample of Scrollduggery," *America*, (Sept. 3, 1966), pp. 227–29. In a recent book, *The Sacred Mushroom and the Cross* (1970), Allegro—who is no longer at Manchester or on the Dead Sea Scrolls committee—goes completely "overboard" in attempting to discredit Judaism and Christianity as disguised fertility cults. By an outrageous use of Sumerian etymologies Allegro finds phallic meanings everywhere in the Bible. Fifteen of Britain's most eminent Semitic philologists—including G. R. Driver, P. R. Ackroyd, G. W. Anderson, James Barr, O. R. Gurney, J. B. Segal, D. Winton Thomas, G. Vermes, and D. J. Wiseman—were constrained to write a letter to the *London Times* (May 26, 1970), denouncing the work as "an essay in fantasy rather than philology."

24. John M. Allegro, *The Treasure of the Copper Scroll*, pp. 110–12, 178.

25. Cross, "The Early History of the Qumran Community," in Freedman, *New Directions*, pp. 74–78.

26. A. Dupont-Sommer, *The Essene Writings from Qumran*, p. 269.

27. H. H. Rowley, "4QpNahum and the Teacher of Righteousness," *JBL*, LXXV (1956), 190.

28. Dupont-Sommer, *The Essene Writings*, p. 266.

29. H. Silberman, "Unriddling the Riddle: A Study in the Structure and Language of the Habakkuk Pesher," *Revue de Qumran*, XII (1961), 358–59, suggests that God is the subject of the verb "he appeared."

30. Dupont-Sommer, *The Essene Writings*, p. 266, fn. 4.

31. Helmer Ringgren, *The Faith of Qumran*, pp. 184–85; Frank M. Cross, *The Ancient Library of Qumran and Modern Biblical Studies*, p. 223, fn. 54; Menahem Mansoor, *The Dead Sea Scrolls*, p. 156.

32. William H. Brownlee, *The Meaning of the Qumran Scrolls for the Bible*, pp. 143–51.

33. Dupont-Sommer, *The Essene Writings*, pp. 107–108.

34. Ethelbert Stauffer, *Jesus and the Wilderness Community at Qumran*, p. 21. Cf. Oscar Cullmann, "The Significance of the Qumran Scrolls for Research into the Beginnings of Christianity," in *The Scrolls and the New Testament*, ed. Krister Stendahl, pp. 31–32.

Chapter Four: Fragments and Circles

1. The following chapter is an expanded version of an article, "Stones, Scripts, and Scholars," which appeared in *Christianity Today*, XIII (Feb. 14, 1969), 8–10, 12–13.

2. Cf. Cyril Aldred, *The Egyptians*, p. 30. Mortimer Wheeler, *Flames over Persepolis*, p. 96, describing a mound in India, reports: "I recall how, on my first visit to the place in 1944, I had to push my way up the narrow approaches through an opposing herd of buffaloes, each carrying a double pannier filled with the valued phosphatic dust of the high mound for use as agricultural top-dressing. The great mound was being, and had long been, systematically undermined and tumbled by the peasantry, ..."

3. M. Avi-Yonah in Vardaman, *The Teacher's Yoke*, p. 48.

4. Over 1700 speeches were attributed to the ten great Greek orators of the Hellenistic age; only 130 are extant. It has been estimated that perhaps three percent of ancient Greek literature has survived.

5. A. Samuel, *The Mycenaeans in History*, p. 101.

6. Robert Adams in *The American Schools of Oriental Research Newsletter*, (Jan. 20, 1969), p. 6. The government of Iraq has requested the Oriental Institute of Chicago to conduct surveys of ancient canal systems. Surveys have been conducted of the area northeast of Baghdad, and more recently in the area of Nippur.

7. Letter of Nov. 14, 1968, to the author.

8. Lapp, "Palestine . . . Mostly Unknown," pp. 122–23.

9. Seton Lloyd, *Mounds of the Near East*, p. 99.

10. Martin A. Beek, *Atlas of Mesopotamia*, map. 2.

11. C. Leonard Woolley, *A Forgotten Kingdom*, p. 20.

12. Sp. Marinatos, "Helike, Thera, Thebai," *Athens Annual of Archaeology*, I (1968), 17.

13. T. Madhloum, "Nineveh, the 1967–1968 Campaign," *Sumer*, XXIV (1968), 46.

14. Material excavated at Byblos from the beginning of the Iron Age is still largely unpublished. In 1970 James Pritchard reached Iron Age levels at the city of Sarepta (Zarephath), between Tyre and Sidon. The excavation has thus far uncovered the remains of houses from the ninth to the seventh centuries B.C. This is the first evidence from Phoenicia itself for the architecture and daily life of the Phoenicians. *Archaeology*, XXIV.1 (1971), 61–63.

15. George Hanfmann, "Archaeology and the Origins of Greek Culture: Notes on Recent Work in Asia Minor," *The Antioch Review*, (spring, 1965), pp. 42–43.

16. Franken, *A Primer of Old Testament Archaeology*, pp. 159–60.

17. Albright, *New Horizons*, p. 3. The 47-acre mound of Ugarit has occupied archaeologists—with an interruption for World War II—in season after season up to the present time since the initial excavation in 1929 over forty years ago. Nineteen seasons of excavation from 1933 to 1970 have still to exhaust the smaller site of Mari.

18. A. Leo Oppenheim, *Ancient Mesopotamia*, p. 140.

19. Lapp, *Biblical Archaeology and History*, p. 84.

20. Even with Greek and Latin manuscripts publication is still quite fragmentary. Dr. William H. Willis, president of the American Society of Papyrologists, estimates that less than one-fifth of the 100,000 pieces of papyri in collections have been examined and identified. *New York Times*, March 19, 1971.

21. Erle Leichty, "A Remarkable Forger," *Expedition*, XII (spring, 1970), 17. Speaking of some cuneiform tablets that turned out to be forgeries, Dr. Leichty says, "As a matter of fact, it is doubtful that anyone had looked at them since Dr. Holt in 1911." *Ibid.*, p. 21. The writer has examined the Aramaic and Mandaic bowls from Nippus in the University Museum, and doubts whether more than two other scholars have looked at them since James Montgomery published the most important of the bowl inscriptions in 1913.

22. Oppenheim, p. 397. The Hittite Hieroglyphic text discovered at Karatepe in southeastern Turkey in 1946 by H. Bossert had still not been published in full when Bossert died in 1962.

23. Cited by I. Cottrell, *The Lost Pharaohs*, p. 181. In 1963 Christiane Desroche-Noblecourt published a small selection of the finds in *Tutankhamen*, a work which includes seventy-five dazzling color photographs of the finds.

24. The excavations at Lachish were tragically cut short by the murder of Starkey in 1938. Miss O. Tufnell, after laboring for twenty years from incomplete records, published a volume on the Bronze Age of Lachish in 1958. The Danish excavations at Shiloh (Seilun) in 1926, 1929, and 1932 were not published in final form because of the death of Hans Kjaer in 1932. In 1969 a final report on the excavation was pieced together and published by M. Buhl and S. Holm-Nielsen.

25. Albright in Vardaman, *The Teacher's Yoke*, p. 30.

26. Cf. Paul Lapp's estimate, *Biblical Archaeology and History*, pp. 83–84: "Roughly only two percent of potentially good archaeological sites in Palestine have been touched, and only in rare instances is more than five percent of a site excavated. If we estimate that perhaps half of the material from excavated sites has actually been published and of that perhaps five to ten percent has a reliable stratigraphic, typological, and analytic base, the amount of trustworthy data available to the historian is an extremely limited sample."

27. Georges Posener, *Leçon Inaugurale*, pp. 10–11.

28. Samuel, p. 82.

29. Dougherty, pp. 13–14.

30. A. Olmstead, "Tattenai, Governor of 'Across the River,'" *JNES*, III (1944), 46.

31. Jerry Vardaman, "A New Inscription which Mentions Pilate as 'Prefect,'" *JBL*, LXXXI (1962), 70–71.

32. Yigael Yadin, *Masada*, p. 189.

33. M. Avi-Yonah, "The Epitaph of T. Mucius Clemens," *IEJ*, XVI (1966), 258–64.

34. We have three accounts of the battle of Der fought in Mesopotamia which give credit for the victory in turn to Sargon, to Merodach-Baladan, and to Humbanigash. Judging from the character of the sources and of the persons involved the probable victor was Humbanigash. Two major Aramaean uprisings in the seventh century B.C. are not mentioned in the official Assyrian texts from Nineveh but are known only from the letters of the period.

35. Hilda Lorimer, *Homer and the Monuments*, pp. 196 ff.

36. Anthony Snodgrass, *Early Greek Armour and Weapons*, p. 71.

37. George Hanfmann, "Archaeology in Homeric Asia Minor," *AJA*, LII (1948), 135–55.

38. Hanfmann, "Archaeology and the Origins of Greek Culture."

39. Gilbert Picard, *The Ancient Civilization of Rome*, p. 86.

40. Albright, *Yahweh and the Gods of Canaan*, p. 235.

41. M. Avi-Yonah in *IEJ*, VI (1956), 196.

42. De Vaux in Sanders, *Near Eastern Archaeology*, p. 70.

43. Review of E. A. Speiser's *Genesis* in *Interpretation*, XIX (1965), 331. Cf. Cyrus H. Gordon, "Higher Critics and Forbidden Fruit," *Christianity Today*, IV (Nov. 23, 1959), 3–6.

44. Cf. W. W. Hallo, "New Viewpoints on Cuneiform Literature," *IEJ*, XII (1962), 14.

45. In Hyatt, *The Bible in Modern Scholarship*, pp. 41–42. Cf. Kitchen, *Ancient Orient and Old Testament*.

46. Wiseman in *AOTS*, p. 122.

Index of Modern Names

(Note: * marks names in chapter notes.)

Ackroyd, P. R., *188
Adams, R., 148
Aharoni, Y., *178, *179, *182
Albright, W. F., 18, 24, 25, 34, 36, 39, 42, 48, 54, 60, 62, 64, 67, 70, 78, 84, 87, 95, 127, 139, 156, 161, 164, *174, *176, *180, *181, *182, *183, *190
Aldred, C., *189
Allegro, J., 133, 140, 141, 142
Alt, A., 29, 31, 50, 52
Anderson, G. W., *188
Archer, G., 49, *177
Avi-Yonah, M., 148, 162, *189, *191

Bagatti, P. B., 121
Baramki, D. C., *185
Barnett, R. D., 70, 80
Barr, J., *188
Bass, G., 152
Baur, F. C., 92, 93
Beebe, H. K., 62
Beegle, D. M., *174
Beek, G. W. van, *180
Beek, M. A., 150
Bickerman, E. J., *182
Biran, A., 71
Black, M., 142
Bossert, H., *190
Bousset, W., 94
Bright, J., 25, 30, *174
Brinkman, J. A., *181
Brown, R. E., 138, 139
Brownlee, W. H., 142, 144
Bruce, F. F., 25, 99, 142, *187
Buhl, M., *191

Bull, R. J., *179
Bultmann, R., 94, 95
Burrows, M., 22, 143

Cadbury, H. J., 119
Callaway, J. A., 60
Campbell, E. F., *178
Carter, H., 155
Champollion, J. F., 147
Chiera, E., 148
Clark, K. W., *187
Clermont-Ganneau, C., 120
Conant, K. J., 112
Conzelmann, H., *184
Corbo, V., 102
Cottrell, L., *190
Cross, F. M., Jr., 25, 131, 134, 142, *176, *182, *187, *189
Cullmann, O., *186, *191

Deismann, A., 118, 120, *185
Deiss, J., *186
Desroche-Noblecourt, C., *190
DeVries, C. E., *177
Dibelius, M., 94, 95
Dinkler, E., *186
Dothan, M., 56
Dougherty, R., 89, *191
Douglas, J. D., *177
Driver, G. R., 142, *188
Driver, S. R., 36, 90
Duhm, B., 65
Dupont-Sommer, A., 44, 140, 142, 143, *189

Eissfeldt, O., 36, 42
Evans, L. E. C., *185

Filson, F. V., *188
Finegan, J., 99, *186
Fishwick, D., *186
Fitzmyer, J. A., *188
Franken, H. J., 72, *190'
Franken-Battershill, C. A., *181
Frankfort, H., 146
Frazer, J., 34
Freedman, D. N., *174, *182, *187, *188
Frova, A., 114

Gadd, C. J., *183
Gardiner, A., 156
Garstang, J., 57, 58, 152, *179
Gasque, W. W., 96, *184
Gauthier, H., 147
Gibson, J. C. L., *175
Glock, A. E., *177
Glueck, N., 37, 39, 40, 48, 49, 69, 149, *180
Gordon, C. H., *176, *192
Gray, J., 58
Grayson, A. K., 90
Greenberg, M., 164, *178
Greenfield, J. C., *175
Gressman, H., 163
Guarducci, M., 125
Gunkel, H., 29, 31, 36
Gurney, O. R., 44, *188
Gustafsson, B., 122

Haas, N., *185
Hahn, H. F., *175
Hallo, W. W., 75, 76, *192
Hamrick, E. W., *185
Hanfmann, G., 161, *190
Haran, M., *178
Harding, G. L., 134
Harnack, A., 96
Haupt, P., 163

Hegel, G. W. F., 28, 92
Heichelheim, F. M., 99
Heidel, A., *175
Hennessy, J. B., *185
Hodgson, P. C., *183
Hoffner, H., 44
Holm-Nielsen, S., *191
Holt, J. M., 45
Hunter, A. M., *188
Hyatt, J. P., *179, *182, *184, *192

James, F. W., 156
Jamme, A., *180
Janssen, J., *177
Jensen, P., 32
Jeremias, A., 36
Jonge, M. de, *188
Jothams-Rothschild, J., 123

Kaiser, W. C., *175
Karrer, O., *186
Kaufmann, Y., 55, *178
Kelso, J., 56, 57, 104, *179, *180
Kenyon, K., 57, 58, 60, 67, 83, 86, 112, *181, *185
Kitchen, K. A., 42, 48, 50, 78, *177, *182, *192
Kittel, R., 163
Kjaer, H., *191
Kochavi, M., 149
Kohl, H., 102
Kramer, S. N., 52, 155
Kuhn, K. G., 143

Lambert, W. G., 32, 90
Landes, G., 163
Landsberger, B., 54
Lapp, P., 58, 62, 149, 153, *179, *191
Lawrence, T. E., 81

Lehmann, M. R., 43
Leichty, E., 154
Livingston, D., *179
Lloyd, S., 149
Lorimer, H. L., 161

Macalister, R. A. S., 68, *185
Madhloum, T., 150
Malamat, A., 70
Mallowan, M., 34, 74, 152, *180
Mansoor, M., *189
Marinatos, S., *190
Marquet-Krause, J., 60
Martin, W. J., *183
Mayer, L. A., 114
Mazar, B., 65, 152
McDonald, W. A., 118
Meek, T., *177
Mendenhall, G. E., 25, 50
Meyer, E., 36, 86, 96
Milik, J. T., 134, 142, *186
Millard, A., 35
Mommsen, T., 98, 120
Montet, P., 48, 49, *176
Munck, J., 93
Myers, J., *183

Naveh, J., *182, *183
Nineham, D. E., *186
Nöldeke, T., 39
North, R., *185
Noth, M., 29, 36, 39, 44, 50, 58, 60, 163, *176

O'Connor, D., *186
Olmstead, A. T., 96, 159
Oppenheim, A. L., 89, 153
Orfali, G., 102
Orlinsky, H., 32

Page, D. L., *175
Parrot, A., 21, 38, 42, 45, 54, 75

Parry, M., 164
Payne, J. B., *175, *177, *183, *187
Perkins, J. W., *186
Pfeiffer, R. H., 30, 65, 81
Picard, G., 161
Posener, G., *191
Power, W. J. A., *177, *178
Pritchard, J. B., 59, 68, 69, *183, *190

Quinn, J. D., *181

Rabinowitz, I., *182
Rad, G. von, 50
Raikes, R., *175
Rainey, A., 59
Ramsay, W., 95, 96, 98, 99
Ratisbonne, A., 106
Rice, D. S., 88
Ringgren, H., *189
Ross, J. F., 57
Roth, C., 142
Rothenberg, B., 37, 69, 149
Rowley, H. H., 36, 87, 88, 142, 143, *176

Saggs, H. W. F., 77
Saller, S. J., 106, *185
Samuel, A., 148, 157
Sanders, J. A., *175, *182, *191
Saulcy, F. de, 134
Sayce, A. H., 30
Segal, J. B., *188
Sellin, E., 18, 58, 64
Selms, A. van, *177
Sherwin-White, A. N., 120
Silberman, H., *189
Simpson, C. A., 36
Skehan, P. W., *187, *188
Smith, G., 33

Smith, M., *175, 66
Smith, S., 88, 89
Snodgrass, A., *191
Snyder, G. F., 125
Sokolowski, F., *185
Speiser, E., 32, 40, 42, 44, 47, *177, *192
Starkey, J. L., *181, *191
Stauffer, E., 145
Steele, F., 52, 154
Stendahl, K., *191
Stubbings, F., *180
Sukenik, E. L., 114, 121, 122, 126, 127, 128, 147
Sutcliffe, E., 142

Taylor, L. R., *184
Taylor, V., 94
Testa, E., *185
Thenius, O., 110
Theron, D. J., *184
Thomas, D. W., *176, *188
Thompson, R. C., 153
Thompson, R. J., *175
Torrey, C. C., 81, 83, 84, 85, 86
Toynbee, J., *186
Trever, J. C., 127
Tsaferis, V., *185
Tucker, G. M., *176
Tufnell, O., *181, *190

Unger, M., 49

Vardaman, J., *188, *189, *191
Vaux, R. de, *25, 36, 44, 54, 71, 128, 134, 142, 162, *175
Vergote, J., *177
Vermes, G., 142, *188
Vermeule, E., 159
Vincent, L. H., 60

Wace, A., *180
Waltke, B., *187
Warmington, B. H., 97
Watzinger, C., 102
Weidner, E., 85
Weill, R., 112
Weinberg, S., *182
Weingreen, J., 87
Wellhausen, J., 28, 29, 30, 65, 92, 163
Wheeler, M., 21, *191
Whitcomb, J., 87
Wilbour, C., 46, 47
Williamson, G. A., 97
Willis, W. H., *190
Wilson, C, 102
Wilson, E., 140
Winckler, H., 36
Wiseman, D. J., 20, 25, 65, 82, 88, *176, *188, *192
Wolf, C. U., *179
Wolf, F. A., 28
Wood, J. T., 118
Wood, L. T., *177
Woolley, L., 34, 39, 150, 156
Wotschitzky, A., *185
Woude, A. S. van der, *188
Wright, G. E., 24, 25, 63, *175, *176, *177, *178, *180, *181

Yadin, Y., 56, 68, 127, 133, 136, 152, 153, *180, *191
Yahuda, A. S., *176
Yamauchi, E., 114, *175, *176, *177, *183, *184, *187, *188
Yaron, R., *177
Yeivin, S., 36, 60
Young, T. C., Jr., 43

Zahn, T., 96
Zeitlin, S, 129

Index of Ancient Names

Aaron, 46
Abimelech, 63
Abraham, 24, 36, 37, 38, 40, 42, 45
Ahab, 68, 72, 73
Akhnaton, 165
Alcaeus, 81
Alexander Jannaeus, 142
Amraphel, 39, 40
Annas, 106
Apollonius of Tyana, 114
Araunah, 44
Aretas, 113
Arioch, 39, 40
Asenath, 47
Asher, 47
Ashurnasirpal II, 67
Augustus, 98

Barak, 63
Bar-Kochba, 152
Barnabas, 115
Barsabbas, 121, 122
Belshazzar, 88, 89, 159
Ben-Hadad, 73, 74
Benjamin, 37

Caiaphas, 106
Cambyses, 86
Chedorlaomer, 39, 40
Claudius, 116
Constantine, 100, 110
Cyrenius (Quirinius), 98, 99
Cyrus the Great, 85, 86, 88, 91

Daniel, 82
Darius the Great, 87, 91

Darius the Mede, 87, 88, 159
David, 44, 64, 65, 164
Deborah, 63

Erastus, 116
Esau, 39
Ezekiel, 82

Felix, 120, 160
Festus, 120

Gallio, 116
Geshem, 86
Gideon, 63
Goliath, 64, 65

Hadrian, 100, 106, 110
Hagar, 38, 39
Hammurabi, 38, 39, 40, 47, 51, 52
Hazael, 73
Helen of Adiabene, 112
Helena, 100
Herod Agrippa I, 111, 112, 113, 114, 115, 122
Herod the Great, 98, 106, 114, 159
Herodotus, 79
Hezekiah, 76, 77, 78, 80
Hiram, 69
Homer, 29, 64, 65, 159, 161, 164
Hoshea, 74, 75
Hyrcanus I, 134

Idrimi, 164
Ishmael, 39

Jacob, 37, 48
James, 48
Jehoahaz (Ahaz), 74
Jehoiachin, 83, 84, 85
Jehoiakim, 82
Jehoshaphat, 73
Jehu, 73
Jeroboam I, 71
Jeroboam II, 74
Jerome, 100
Jesus, 122
Jezebel, 72
Joash, 73
John the Baptist, 99, 137
Joram, 73
Joseph, 46, 47, 48
Joseph of Arimathea, 111
Josephus, 97, 111, 122, 136, 142
Joshua, 56, 57, 58, 59, 60, 62
Josiah, 81, 90
Julian, 114
Justin Martyr, 100

Laban, 37, 45
Lazarus, 105, 121, 122
Lipit-Ishtar, 52, 154
Luke, 96, 98, 99, 115, 119
Lydia, 115
Lysanias, 99

Mark Antony, 106
Martha (sister of Lazarus), 121, 122
Mary (sister of Lazarus), 122
Mary (mother of Jesus), 100
Melchizedek, 139
Melito, 100
Menahem, 47, 74
Merari, 46
Merneptah, 48, 56
Merodach-Baladan, 80

Mesha, 72, 73, 147
Moses, 29, 46

Nabonidus, 87, 88, 89, 159
Nahor, 37
Nebuchadnezzar, 81, 82, 83, 87, 90, 91
Necho, 81, 82, 90
Nehemiah, 86, 87
Nero, 116, 120
Nicanor, 123

Omri, 72, 73
Origen, 100

Pashhur, 46
Paul, 112 ff.
    burial, 125
    conversion, 113
Pekah, 74
Peter, 102, 124, 125
Philo, 120, 136
Phinehas, 46
Pilgrim of Bordeaux, 100, 105, 110
Pliny the Elder, 136
Pompey, 113, 144
Pontius Pilate, 42, 106, 108, 159
Potiphar, 47
Psammetichus I, 90

Rachel, 39
Ramesses II, 48, 49, 160
Ramesses III, 45
Rehoboam, 71
Rezin, 74

Sapphira, 121, 122
Sarah, 38
Sargon II, 75, 76, 80, 160
Saturninus, 99

Saul, 64, 65
Seneca, 116
Sennacherib, 76, 77, 78, 79, 80
Serug, 37
Shalmaneser III, 73
Shalmaneser V, 74, 75, 160
Shiphrah, 47
Shishak, 71
Siamun, 70
Silas, 115
Sisera, 63
Solomon, 49, 67, 68, 69, 70, 71
Stephen, 113

Tatnai, 159
Terah, 37
Tertullian, 99

Theodotus, 113
Tidal, 38, 39
Tiglath-Pileser III, 74, 77
Timothy, 115
Tirhakah, 78
Titus, 100, 111
Trophimus, 120
Tutankhamon, 155

Ur-Nammu, 52

Xerxes, 91

Zacchaeus, 104
Zakir, 74
Zedekiah, 83
Zimri, 71

Index of Places

Abila, 99
Abusir, 157
Adab, 155
Ai, 57, 60, 62, 152, 153
Alalakh, 39, 65, 164
Amman, 49
Ammon, 48
Antioch, 114
Arabah Valley, 40, 69
Arabia, 113
Arad, 61, 153
Arbela, 150
Ashdod, 56, 76, 153
Ashkelon (revise spelling from
  Askalon), 56, 148, 153
Assur, 153

Baalbek, 156
Babylon, 77, 88, 91, 147, 153,
  154
Bethany, 105, 121
Bethel, 56, 60, 62, 71
Bethesda, 103, 104
Bethlehem, 100
Beth-shan (revise spelling from
  Beth-shean), 57, 64, 156
Byblos, 147

Caesarea, 114, 119, 147, 148,
  159, 160
Calah (see Nimrud),
Cana, 100, 102
Capernaum, 102
Carchemish, 81, 82
Carthage, 161
Chorazin, 102
Corinth, 116, 118

Cyprus, 119

Damascus, 73, 74, 113, 150
Dan, 71
Dead Sea, 41
Debir, 57
Delphi, 116, 150
Dendra, 161
Der, *191
Derbe, 115, 151
Dothan, 153
Dur-Sharrukin, 153

Edom, 48
Egypt, 150
En-Gedi, 152
Ephesus, 118, 119, 151
Eridu, 152
Ezion-Geber, 69

Gaza, 151
Gerizim, 103
Gezer, 68, 70, 153
Gibeah, 64
Gibeon, 57, 59, 60, 61, 152, 153
Gilboa, 64
Gomorrah, 39, 134

Halicarnassus, 152
Haran, 37, 38, 88, 89
Hattusha, 153
Hazor, 56, 61, 62, 68, 74, 153
Herculaneum, 123

Iconium, 115, 151
Ilahun, 157
Iraq, 150

Jabesh-Gilead, 64
Jericho, 57, 58, 60, 62, 104, 105, 136, 146, 152, 153
Jerusalem, 67, 77, 78, 79, 82, 83, 86, 100, 103, 105, 106, 111, 112 area, 114, 115
    Dominus Flevit, 121, 122
    Fortress Antonia, 120
    size, 114, 115
    Talpioth, 121, 122
    walls, 114
Judaea, 41

Kadesh, 160
Kishon, 64

Lachish, 62, 80, 83, 153
Lystra, 115, 151

Malta, 119
Mari, 38, 40, 42, 65, 155, *175
Mars Hill, 116
Masada, 102, 147, 151
Megiddo, 57, 63, 68, 71, 81, 151, 152, 153
Moab, 48, 72, 73

Nazareth, 100, 148
Negeb, 37
Nile, 46
Nimrud, 67, 68, 74, 77, 152
Nineveh, 80, 81, 150, 153, 155
Nippur, 154, 155
Nuzi, 38, 39

Ophir, 70

Phaistos, 156
Philadelphia, 151

Philippi, 115
Pompeii, 123

Qarqar, 72
Qumran, 65, 66, 67, 134, 151

Raamses, 48
Ramat Rahel, 82
Rome, 161

Samaria, 72, 75, 104
Saqqara, 81
Shechem, 57, 63
Sidon, 150
Siloam, 76, 103
Sinai, 37
Smyrna, 151
Sodom, 39

Taanach, 57, 63, 64
Tanis, 49
Tarshish, 70
Tell Asmar, 155
Tell Beit Mirsim, 57, 152, 153
Tell el-Ajjul, 153
Tema, 88
Thebes (Greece), 150
Thessalonica, 115, 116
Thyatira, 151
Tirzah, 72
Trans-Jordan, 149
Tyre, 150

Ugarit, 66, 67, *190
Ur, 34, 37, 38, 45
Uruk, 153

Zakro, 151
Zarethan, 69

Subject Index

Adonis, 100
Ahiqar, 90
Akkadian, 163
Amarna Letters, 44, 54, 71
Anachronisms, 40-42
Aramaeans, 44-45
Aramaic, 45, 77, 81, 86, 90
Artemis, 118
Assyrians, 72, 73, 74, 77, 80, 90
Atrahasis Epic, 35

Bishops, 138, 139

Calvary, 108, 110, 111
Camels, 42, 43
Cenacle, 106
Chaldaeans, 45, 80
Coins, 129, 157
Conquest of Canaan, 48, 49, 50, 54, 55, 62
Copper Mines, 69
Copper Scroll, 133
Cross, 122, 123
Crucifixion, 143

Damascus Document, 132, 141
Diana, 118, 119
Documentary Hypothesis, 28

Ecce Homo Arch, 106
Egyptian, 46, 47, 48
Elephantine Papyri, 86
Enuma Elish, 31
Eshnunna Law Code, 52, 53
Essenes, 136, 140, 143, 144, 145
Evangelicals, 25

Exodus
Date of, 48, 49, 54

Flood, 33, 34, 35
Form Criticism, 29, 94, 95
Fundamentalism, 23, 24

Garden Tomb, 108, 110
Genesis Apocryphon, 131
German Scholarship, 25, 36
Gilgamesh Epic, 32, 33, 34, 35
Good Samaritan, 105
Greek(s), 75, 81, 86, 97, 90, 91

Habakkuk Commentary, 132, 141
Habiru, 54
Hermes, 115
Higher Criticism, 27
"History of Religions" School, 93, 94
Hittites, 43, 44
Holy Sepulchre, 108, 110, 111, 112
Horites, 44
Hurrians, 44

King James Version, 70, 130

Lachish Ostraca, 83
Linear B, 159
Literary Criticism, 163, 164

Maccabean, 91
Mandaeans, 94
Manual of Discipline, 132

Masoretic Text, 129, 130
Medes, 43, 87, 88
Messiah, 141, 142
Moloch, 161
Mystery Religions, 94, 139
Nabataeans, 113

Nahum Commentary, 142
Neo-Babylonians, 80, 81
Nubian, 46

Ossuaries, 121

Papyri, 147, 157
Patriarchs, 36 ff.
Persians, 43, 81, 84, 85, 87, 88
Philistines, 45, 46, 56, 64, 65
Phoenicians, 69, 70, 72, 161
Prophecy, 91

Radio-carbon Dating, 129
Redactional History Scholars, 94, 95
Revised Standard Version, 130
Roads, 105, 106

Samaritan Recension, 131
Septuagint, 44, 130, 131
Slaves, Price of, 47
St. Peter's Church, 124
Statues, 157
Synagogues, 102, 113, 118, 147

Tammuz, 100
Teacher of Righteousness, 132, 140, 142, 143, 144, 145, 165
Temple Scroll, 133
Ten Commandments, 52
Thanksgiving Hymns, 132, 141, 144
Traditions, 159, 160
Tübingen School, 92, 94, 95

Ugaritic, 66, 163, 164

Via Egnatia, 115

War Scroll, 132

Zadokite Document, 132
Zeus, 115

Index of Scriptures

GENESIS

1:1   32
8:21-9:1   35
10:2   43
14   24, 40, 139
15:2   38
15:20   43
20-21   45
23:3   43
25:20   45
28:5   45
31:20, 24   45
31:47   45
37:28   47
39:1   47
41:1   46
41:41   47
41:45   48

EXODUS   130

1:11   48, 50
1:15   47
6:16   46
12:40   36
20   50
21:35   52

LEVITICUS

18:21   161

NUMBERS

12:1   46

DEUTERONOMY

8:3   20
26:5   45

JOSHUA

11:1-13   56
15:16 ff.   57
17:11-12   57
24:2   37
24:24   50

JUDGES

1   54
1:27   63
4-5   63
5:21   64
9   63

I SAMUEL   131

1:3   46
10:5   64
13:19-22   64
17:6   65
24:4   65
31:12-13   64

I KINGS

6:1   49, 50
7:45-46   69
8:65   67
9:15   67
9:15-19   68
9:16   70
9:24   67
9:26   69
10:22-24   70
10:28   70
14:25-26   71
16:23   72
22:39   72

II KINGS

3:5   73
3:27   73
10:32   73
13:24-25   73
15:19 ff.   74
15:29   74
15:30 ff.   74
16:1-6 74
17:3-6 75
17:6   160
18-19   78
18:10   75, 160
18:13   78
18:26   77
19:9   78
20:12-18   80
20:20   76
23-24   81
23:10   161
23:29   81
24:1   82
24:17   83
25:27-30   85

II CHRONICLES

8:17-18 69
9:10-11 70
9:21-22 70
32:30   76
32:31   80
36:10   83

EZRA   86

1:2-4   86
2:69   86
4:8-6:18   81
5:3   159
5:6   159
6:2   86

6:3-5   86
7:12-26 81
8:27   86

NEHEMIAH

2:19   86
6:1-2   86
6:6   86
7:70-72 86

ESTHER   129

PSALMS   65, 67, 164

PROVERBS 66

ISAIAH   130

20:1   75
36-37   78
37:9   78
39:1-8 80

JEREMIAH 131

7:30-31 161
20:1   46
22:13 ff.   82
34:7   83
37:6 ff.   82
49:28   86

EZEKIEL 84

40-48   139

DANIEL   87 ff., 91, 159

1:1   82
4:32   89
5:29   88

AMOS

9:7   45

MATTHEW

4:4   20

MATTHEW (*continued*)

5:43   144
23:2   102

LUKE

2:2   98
3:1   99
10:30   105

JOHN   94, 137, 138

3:12   21
4   103
5:1-14   104
9:7-11   103
19:13   108

ACTS   92, 95, 97, 120

1:23   121
2   113
2-5   138
5   121
6:9   112
11:26   114
12   114
12:23   114
13:7   119
14:6   115
14:12   115
16:12   115
17:6   115
17:23   116
18:4   118
18:12-17   116
19:22   116

19:24 ff.   118
19:29-31   118
19:31   119
21:27-30   120
25:26   120
26:13   113
28:7   119

ROMANS

16:23   118

I CORINTHIANS

1:26   118

II CORINTHIANS

11:32   113

GALATIANS

1:17   113
2:1-10   93

EPHESIANS

2:14   120

I TIMOTHY   139

II TIMOTHY   139

TITUS   139

HEBREWS   139, 140

1-2   139
7:3   139

REVELATION   139

1:8   124